William Charles Cotton MA
1813 - 1879

Priest, Missionary and Bee Master

To my parents who gave me a good start in life

William Charles Cotton MA
1813 - 1879

Priest, Missionary and Bee Master

Arthur R Smith

Countyvise

First Published 2006 by Countyvise Limited,
14 Appin Road, Birkenhead, Wirral CH41 9HH.

Copyright © 2006

The right of Arthur R Smith to be identified as the author of this work has been asserted by him in accordance with the Copyright, Design and Patents Act 1988.

British Library Cataloguing in Publication Data.
A catalogue record for this book is available from the British Library.

Please note: From 1st January 2007 ISBNs will contain 13 numbers these numbers will be the same as the present number printed below the barcode (ie. starting 978).
Countyvise is showing both existing (10 digit) and future (13 digit) ISBNs on the Title page verso. Please continue to use the 10 figure number until 31st December 2006.

ISBN 1 901231 81 X   ISBN 978 1 901231 81 X

All rights reserved. No part of this publication may be reproduced, stored in a retrieval system, or transmitted, in any other form, or by any other means, electronic, chemical, mechanic, photocopying, recording or otherwise, without the prior permission of the publisher.

William Charles Cotton MA
1813 - 1879
Priest, Missionary and Bee Master

CONTENTS

Sponsorship	4
Acknowledgements	4
Preface	6
Introduction	7
Chapter 1 The Formative Years	9
Chapter 2 The Voyage to New Zealand	32
Chapter 3 The Waimate Mission Station	65
Chapter 4 Life at the Waimate	82
Chapter 5 The Move to Auckland	134
Chapter 6 Return to England - The Lost Years	160
Chapter 7 Vicar of Frodsham - 1857 to 1879	171
Chapter 8 The Grand Bee Master, Home Life, Church Schools and Final Days	197
Glossary of Maori Words	212
Appendices	214
Bibliography	221
Index	225

William Charles Cotton MA
1813 - 1879
Priest, Missionary and Bee Master

Sponsorship

I wish to thank the following individuals and organizations for their generous contribution towards meeting the costs of this publication:

The Frodsham Town Council

St Laurence Parochial Church Council, Frodsham

The Vice Provost of Eton College

Devonshire Bakery

Christ Church, Oxford

Acknowledgements

In a work of this kind, which has taken many years of research, there are a large number of people whose help has been invaluable. In particular I would like to thank the following:

(i)   Mrs Judith Curthoys, Archivist, of Christ Church, Oxford.
(ii)   Miss Elizabeth Stratton, Archivist, of Selwyn College, Cambridge, and the former Archivist, Ms Sophie Bridges.
(iii)   Ms Rachel M Rowe, Smuts Librarian for South African and Commonwealth Studies, Cambridge University Library.
(iv)   The Search Room staff at the Cheshire Record Office, Chester.
(v)   Ms Josephine Parker, Archivist, Waltham Forest Archives and Local Studies Library.
(vi)   Mr T and Mr Chris Cotton for their helpful advice and suggestions.
(vii)   The late Mrs Phyllis Hill for the translation of Latin mottoes and inscriptions.

William Charles Cotton MA
1813 - 1879
Priest, Missionary and Bee Master

(viii)   Mr H F Starkey of Runcorn, historian, who has given me much valuable advice and encouragement.

(ix)   Dr Neville Thompson for his meticulous proof reading of the manuscript.

(x)   Stuart Crook, Anita Boardman, Andrew Faraday and Peter Swift for their assistance with word processing, scanning images and allied matters.

(xi)   Mr John Webster of Auckland who supplied me with my first books on The Waimate and later made some useful suggestions for further reading.

(xii)   Reverend R J Draper, Vicar of St John the Baptist Church, Leytonstone and Mrs April Ingham of Frodsham for help with photographs of the church in Leytonstone.

(xiii)   Mr Bill Chapman of Deganwy, North Wales, for his generous gift of various documents without which a large section of Chapter Seven could never have been completed.

(xiv)   Mrs Doreen Wilding, Senior Library Assistant, and her staff at Frodsham Public Library for their help in obtaining source material.

(xv)   Mrs Christine Dunne for her kind assistance with a number of photographs.

(xvi)   Mrs Angela Greene for her help with the maps.

(xvii)   My wife, Kay, for her patience and positive comments, when over the last few months I have read practically the whole manuscript to her.

Arthur R Smith September 2006

William Charles Cotton MA
1813 - 1879
Priest, Missionary and Bee Master

Preface

That old cliché suggests that there is a book inside each one of us – but for most of us that book never comes out.

It is a privilege to be asked to write a few words as a preface to this book. I might know something about what it means to be Vicar of Frodsham in the 21st Century – but Cotton's world was just so different! And I have to say I knew nothing about bees – apart from the fact that as you walk round our lovely town there are signs and symbols that point to something of the legacy left by Cotton.

Martin Luther King said, "If a man is called to be a street sweeper, he should sweep streets even as Michelangelo painted or Beethoven composed music or Shakespeare wrote poetry. He should sweep streets so well that all the hosts of heaven and earth will pause to say: "here lived a great street sweeper who did his job well."

So it is wonderful that Arthur has produced this life story with such love and devotion and made this man, with all his ups and downs, come alive. In both cases they have done their job well.

Reverend Michael Mills
The Vicarage, Frodsham
September 2006.

William Charles Cotton MA
1813 - 1879
Priest, Missionary and Bee Master

Introduction

The Reverend William Charles Cotton, vicar of St Laurence Church, Frodsham, Cheshire, from 1857 to 1879, was one of the most interesting characters in the town's history. Throughout his life he had a great passion for bees and bee keeping. In 1841 he sailed with Dr George Selwyn who had been appointed as the first Church of England Bishop of New Zealand. There is a long-standing belief that he took with him the first honeybees ever to reach those distant shores. As we shall see this now seems most unlikely. Nevertheless he did play a full part in helping to establish the Anglican Church in New Zealand, not to mention his considerable work in spreading the best practices in beekeeping among settlers and Maori alike.

One of the main sources of information for Cotton's life in New Zealand is the set of journals which he kept mainly for the benefit of his family. As each volume was finished, it was sent to his sisters in England. Unfortunately the second volume, which covered his voyage from Sydney to the Bay of Islands and his first three months at Waimate, is missing.
The remaining journals No.s 1, and from No.s 3 to 12 are in the Dixson Library, The State Library of New South Wales, Sydney, but fortunately for historians in England there are microfilm copies available in this country.
The journals are profusely illustrated and were in some cases written up from his rough notes. The pencil sketches are by his fellow missionaries, principally William Bambridge and Thomas Biddulph Hutton. Pictures of Cotton himself, and of Europeans and Maori connected with the mission occur throughout the journals.

After years of vigorous activity in New Zealand, there is some mystery about how Cotton spent the next ten years of his life. Similarly it is difficult to know exactly how he felt when, in 1857, he took the living at Frodsham. Perhaps he expected to lead a quiet life in a sleepy rural backwater. Instead he found himself in charge of a very large parish of eight townships, two of which had recently established their own churches whilst others were soon to follow suit. To make matters worse the parish church had fallen into a dilapidated and gloomy state that demanded a radical overhaul to bring it into a condition befitting the needs of the modern community. These, and other problems - not least his own state of health - presented Vicar Cotton with a huge challenge. To what extent he succeeded, despite his personal difficulties, will become evident as the narrative unfolds.

Finally, in spite of his faults, there has been no other vicar, and indeed probably no other person, who is so well remembered in the public mind in Frodsham. The honey bee symbol appears on the Chain of Office of the Town Mayor, the badge of the Manor House County Primary School, on the blue plaques on historic buildings and even on the new bollards and litter bins in the centre of the town. His connection with New Zealand is recalled in at least one street name, Maori Drive, and by the inscription "Haere Maie Te Manuwiri" (Welcome Stranger from Afar) which can still be seen on the doorstep of the Old Vicarage.

William Charles Cotton MA
1813 - 1879
Priest, Missionary and Bee Master

CHAPTER ONE

THE FORMATIVE YEARS

Early Life, School and University, Father's Influence, Interest in Bee-keeping, George Selwyn and New Zealand

William Charles Cotton is remembered mostly for his ability and prowess as a beekeeper and as the author of a number of books on apiculture. He had become interested in bees at an early age. It is said that one day his father read him a passage from Virgil about bees. The next morning he tried to persuade his father's farming man to slaughter a two-year-old calf to enable him to get a swarm of bees from the maggots when the carcass decomposed. His father, hearing of his son's desperate and unrealistic plan, quickly obtained his first hive for him. From these early beginnings Cotton developed a great skill and expertise in bee keeping. By the time of his student days at Oxford he had acquired a remarkable dexterity and affinity with bees. It is said he was able to keep and handle a bee in his trouser pocket.

Born on 30th January 1813, William Charles was the first child of William and Sarah Cotton, who lived at Walwood House, Leytonstone, Essex. His father had prospered in business and was soon to become a Governor of the Bank of England. Their large mansion was set in extensive grounds, befitting one of the gentry. His mother had seven children but her third son died at the age of eighteen. William Charles had three brothers, Henry, Joseph Edward and Arthur Benjamin and three sisters, Sarah, Phoebe and Agnes. In view of his close relationship

William Charles Cotton MA
1813 - 1879
Priest, Missionary and Bee Master

with his sisters in later life, it is reasonable to suppose that he enjoyed a happy childhood with his brothers and sisters at Walwood House.

His parents were good hosts at Walwood and during WCC's childhood many notable persons visited the house. When her uncle, John Cotton, who lived in India, sought a home in England for his eight children, Mrs Cotton offered to have them stay. Clearly it was an unselfish and well-ordered home, where with the help of the servants, it was not too difficult to cope with such a large addition to the household. Furthermore it is said that everything the children undertook their parents expected them to perform well. For example, when Sarah took up her needlework her mother checked every stitch before the needle pierced the fabric. Although extremely strict and particular, everyone spoke of Mrs Cotton as a caring and loving mother. However, it should be remembered that WCC probably spent much of his childhood in the care of nurses and governesses.

As far as we know the whole of his early education was provided by tutors at home. Then, at the age of 12 years, he was sent to the Parsonage at Epsom to be given tuition by the Reverend W Mayd, prior to his attending Eton College. His father, writing from Leytonstone, warned him that at Eton he would face more temptations than at a small private school. "However," he wrote, "you will have much greater opportunity for improvement and will be required to exercise principles of self denial and determination to do what you know to be right." Undoubtedly William Cotton believed it was his duty to lay down strict moral guidelines for his son and his letters to Epsom are full of these earnest sentiments. He declared: "Let me recommend you to cultivate a strict integrity of character, never to say what is not true and correct, even in jest." At the same time he said he did not expect his son to be free from faults and that, from time to time, he would get into difficulties, but he hoped William Charles would not hesitate to discuss problems with him. Evidently William Cotton was a firm and high-principled father, but not one to show a great deal of affection towards his son.

In December 1826 he wrote requesting WCC to return home on the coming Friday when, he said, "we shall have the pleasure of seeing you."[1] As the boy was due to go to Eton early in the New Year, his father declared that he should stop off in London to order what he needed - presumably books and clothes for his new school. In the ensuing months the fourteen year old made a promising start at the College and in the summer of 1827, his father wrote to say that he had received "a gratifying letter" from the boy's tutor, Mr Chapman, reporting that he had conducted himself satisfactorily during his first six months.

In his final year at Eton, he won the Newcastle Prize for excellence in divinity and the classics. The Duke of Newcastle had established this award in 1829. Winners of the Prize received a scholarship that paid an annual amount throughout their university careers.

The Eton College Leaver's Portrait of William Charles Cotton, aged nineteen, painted by Margaret Carpenter in 1832.

It was the custom for boys when leaving to give their portraits to the College.

By kind permission of the Provost and Fellows of Eton College.

William Charles Cotton MA
1813 - 1879
Priest, Missionary and Bee Master

Very little more is known of Cotton's time at Eton, except for one other reference to him in the College annals. In 1831 he was one of the finalists, with a boy called Mellish, in the double sculling. Early in 1832, he left the College with a fine scholastic record, whilst at the same time showing ability in rowing.

On 29th March of the same year, at the age of 19, he matriculated to Christ Church, Oxford. From the time he arrived at the University he held the position of Student (that is, Fellow) of the College. This meant that he received a pension from Christ Church and, provided he took his degrees, remained unmarried and did not take a remunerative post, he could keep this status indefinitely. In his academic studies he showed great ability in mathematics. He gained his BA in 1836, with first class honours in Classics and second class honours in Mathematics. Not a great deal more is known of his undergraduate years, except for his bee-keeping activities and some aspects of his personal life, which are described below.

Tom Quadrangle, Christ Church, Oxford.
(Photograph by kind permission of Derek Langley).

William Charles Cotton MA
1813 - 1879
Priest, Missionary and Bee Master

One of his friends and contemporaries at Christ Church was Henry Acland who, in 1846, married Cotton's sister, Sarah, and went on to become Regius Professor of Medicine at Oxford. In his memoir on Sir Henry Wentworth Acland, J B Atlay states that Cotton was well known "among his fellows for his overflowing animal spirits and inexhaustible fund of humour."[2] Once on a visit to the Acland family home at Holnicote, he was given a room near to that of the housekeeper, Mrs Fletcher. Every morning at daybreak, he used to open his window and crow like a cock much to the annoyance of the old lady. She became so exasperated that she complained to Leopold Acland, whose guest he was, that none of his brothers had ever brought such a "riotous-like" gentleman to Sir Thomas's house before.

Soon after graduation Cotton decided on a career in the church and, in December 1836, he was appointed as a curate at Baston in the diocese of Lincoln. However after a short time he relinquished the curacy and returned to Oxford to continue his studies for his MA.

St. John the Baptist Church, Baston

During these years one of his problems appears to have been the management of his financial affairs. In a succession of letters his father complained that he needed to take greater care with his expenditure, to spend his allowance wisely and avoid falling into debt. However it is difficult to know whether Cotton's extravagant spending was commonplace among students of his day or whether his problem was worse than most of his fellows.

Certainly his father, who had many years experience in business, believed that his son's handling of financial matters was poor and that he needed to exercise a lot more care. In February 1837 William Cotton once again expressed great concern about the state of his son's finances. In one of his letters he listed the sums that WCC had received and the various items of his expenditure. He concluded: "if you have again made a mistake, I had rather again set matters right than see you struggling with uncertainties and difficulties. The great secret, I fear, you have yet to learn is not to purchase anything you do not really require until all necessaries are paid for and there is a surplus in the exchequer........."[3]

In addition to these strictures, his father had become anxious about his son's state of health and other aspects of his conduct. Writing in April 1837 he sympathized with him for the times when he had made mistakes and missed opportunities. He wrote: "I did not say much to you when you were at home on the subject of your depression, altho' I was sorry to observe it."[4] He then expressed serious doubts about whether William Charles had been wise to continue his studies after graduation. In fact, he suggested, it might have been better if he had occupied himself with the practical work of a clergyman. He had only agreed to him staying at Oxford because he hoped his son would have the opportunity to mix in more intellectual company than he would have done as a curate.

During this time a large part of Cotton's postgraduate studies were directed towards his ordination in the Anglican Church. According to the Oxford Diocesan Registers, he was ordained as deacon on 17th December 1837 and as priest on 22nd December 1839. He gained his MA in 1838, and then, in 1839 he took the post of curate of St Edward's Church, Romford, Essex

William Charles Cotton MA
1813 - 1879
Priest, Missionary and Bee Master

William Cotton, Senior

Many years before, his father had also had a strong inclination to enter the Church, but, after much careful thought, he decided to go into business. He soon prospered and eventually became an eminent London businessman, who for a time served as a Governor of the Bank of England.

Walwood House, Leytonstone, the Cotton family home, as it appeared in 1892. Sadly the house was demolished in 1905. Photograph by kind permission of Vestry House Museum London Borough of Waltham Forest.

Born on 12th September 1786, William Cotton attended the Chigwell Grammar School. In 1807 he was admitted as a partner in the firm of Huddert & Co at Limehouse who were engaged in the manufacture of cords and ropes for ships' rigging. He was first elected a Director of the Bank of England in 1822, an office that he held until a few months before his death. From 1843 to 1845 he served as a Governor of the Bank. A permanent memorial to him is preserved in the form of the automatic weighing machine for gold sovereigns, which he invented. He became High Sheriff of Essex in 1837 and for many

William Charles Cotton MA
1813 - 1879
Priest, Missionary and Bee Master

years he served as a magistrate and for a time as Chairman of the Quarter Sessions at Chelmsford.

William Cotton had been a founder of the Church of England National Society, which did so much in the nineteenth century for the provision of schools for the poor. For fifty years he served as the Treasurer of the SPCK - the Society for the Promotion of Christian Knowledge. During his life he helped to build a considerable number of churches in London, two of which were St Thomas's, Bethnal Green (1844) and St Paul's, on Bow Common, Stepney (1847). Both these churches had a special connection to the family. The former he built in memory of his son, Joseph Edward, who died on 6th February 1842 and at the latter church his third son, Arthur Benjamin, became the first incumbent.

William Cotton died on 12th January 1866 aged 80. Such was his devotion to the Church that many of his contemporaries regarded him as one of the saints of his age. It is also said that he was a man of great humility, as he always gave credit to what others had achieved and made little of his own contribution.

Shortly after his death the family arranged for a memorial window to be placed in St Paul's Cathedral, London. In December 1866 it was installed at the east end of the South Aisle of the Choir. Sadly this precious stained glass window was destroyed, along with many others, during the bombing of the city in the Second World War.

William Charles Cotton MA
1813 - 1879
Priest, Missionary and Bee Master

*St John the Baptist's Church, Leytonstone,
for which William Cotton (senior) was a substantial benefactor in 1833.
Photograph by kind permission of Vestry House Museum,
London Borough of Waltham Forest.*

William Cotton appears to have been a typical Victorian upper middle class father who exercised a great deal of influence over his son. Not only did William Charles have a strict upbringing but his father continued to demand obedience well into his early manhood. At the same time, on a number of occasions, he helped his son with generous donations; for instance, he sometimes paid the stipends of curates during the early part of Cotton's incumbency in Frodsham.

Beekeeping

During his undergraduate years William Charles began to develop his youthful interest in beekeeping. In 1833 he helped to found the Oxford Apiarian Society, taking on the office of Secretary. After much hard work in this position, he ventured into print in 1837 with "A Short and Simple Letter to Cottagers from a Bee Preserver." In this pamphlet he gave some sound advice to country folk on how to look after their bees and above all urging them to adopt his humane method of obtaining the honey without harming the bees. Three years later he had a second "Letter" printed, in which he offered more good advice and, incidentally, recorded how he had sold 24,000 copies of the first pamphlet.

In the early 1840s he was ready to set down in full his latest ideas on beekeeping and produced his well-known work "My Bee Book." This manual included his two previous "Letters to Cottagers," along with mottoes about bees, a preface, and extracts from other writers, as well as items from his own Notebook. One of his main ideas in these publications was to persuade cottagers to abandon the brimstone pit as a way of collecting honey. This traditional method involved setting fire to sulphurous rags in a small pit, placing the hive over it and allowing the fumes to asphyxiate the bees, enabling the beekeeper to cut out the combs in safety. Instead of this cruel and wasteful practice, Cotton advocated an alternative plan, namely to stupefy the bees with fumes produced by burning puff balls or puff fungus. Once they were rendered semi-conscious, the bees could be shaken out of the hive, the honey collected and then the bees returned to their home. Later in the day another full hive could be fumigated and the bees from the combless hive introduced into it.[5]

William Charles Cotton MA
1813 - 1879
Priest, Missionary and Bee Master

Cotton, on the left, tending his bees - page 356
"My Bee Book" London 1842.

As one would expect of a Christian minister, "My Bee Book" is liberally sprinkled with exhortations based upon his religious beliefs. He urges that one of the best ways to help the poor is for them to take up beekeeping. He maintains that a stock of bees is better for the poor cottager than a small allotment of land because hard by the allotment is the beer shop. Whereas the busy man tending his bees at home is not so tempted. In winter he can spend time making hives for himself and to sell. "Again his Bee-hives are close to his cottage door and he will learn to like their sweet music better than the dry squeaking of a pot-house fiddle."[6]

In his second "Letter to Cottagers" WCC exhorts his readers to study the Bible first and then, using its principles to guide them, to study nature itself. "Take the Bible and read it through; study it carefully, with prayer to God for the light of his Holy Spirit, and then with its pages in your hand, and its spirit in your heart, turn to the book of nature."[7]

William Charles Cotton MA
1813 - 1879
Priest, Missionary and Bee Master

After a short time at St Edward's Church, Romford, Cotton moved to Windsor Parish Church, where he became a close friend of George Augustus Selwyn, a fellow curate but five years his senior. Without doubt Dr Selwyn and his wife found Cotton to be highly intelligent, capable and kind, but Mrs Selwyn noted how he was given to moods of very high or very low spirits. She describes him as "cheery and lively but an anxiety, truly, from time to time."

During these first few months at Windsor his father was still expressing concern about his son's financial affairs. He declared that William Charles must never again overdraw his account or he would have his cheques returned. It is apparent from his letters that, though William Cotton did not wish to harm his relationship with his son, he was fast losing patience with him. He bemoaned the wild and extravagant behaviour that his son was exhibiting. He declared "I humbly trust that it has pleased God in his mercy at last to awaken you to the folly of your conduct and at our distress at your proceedings, and your painful illness." His father concluded with the hope that, with God's blessing and with his own persevering efforts, his son would overcome his "bad and dissipated habits." Finally he stated, "I hope you have commenced in Mr Selwyn's book, a register of your daily expenses."[8] Once again the main cause of his father's concern was Cotton's inability to exercise a proper degree of restraint over his spending.

It is also clear that throughout the early part of his curacy at Windsor, he was still suffering from spells of depression. At the same time his father was urging him to guard against becoming over excited and pleading with him to cultivate that "composed deportment that is essential in a clergyman."[9] By August 1839 Cotton had become more settled and his numerous duties were keeping him busy. For once he earned his father's praise. "I am very, very happy to see you so usefully and actively engaged with such persons as Selwyn and others around you" he wrote. But even on this occasion he could not resist adding a word of caution - "but we must combine prudence with zeal."[10]

William Charles Cotton MA
1813 - 1879
Priest, Missionary and Bee Master

In March 1840 William Cotton was showing even greater concern at his son's constant state of excitement and of his apparent lack of self-control. "The multiplicity of your pursuits and the intensity with which you follow them up, give the impression you are rather a creature of impulse.........
You and every other clergyman should be distinguished by your quiet, unostentatious but zealous discharge of your ministerial and pastoral duties. Other objects and external pursuits should never be prominent. He added that the publication of those "little entertaining books" - presumably Cotton's "Letters to Cottagers" - should have been left to the Society. Later in the letter he urged his son to model himself on Dr Selwyn. "Why is our friend, Selwyn, so much looked up to and so useful? Not merely for his ability and high principles but because he does not compromise himself with indiscretions. Make him your unreserved friend. He will guide you much better than I can."[11]

In April his father once again complained about his behaviour. He wrote: "in continuation of what I have said about indiscretions, I must however notice the silly and objectionable song you have sent to Sarah. It was throwing away money and the encouraging of such a publication is not very consistent with the duty of honouring the Queen. It is not suitable for a young woman or fit to be in a gentleman's house."[12]

However in the late summer of 1841 a remarkable development took place at Windsor Parish Church that caused William Cotton (senior) to change his attitude completely. George Selwyn, Cotton's fellow curate, was appointed to be the first Anglican Bishop of New Zealand. After giving the matter careful thought, WCC made a momentous decision. He resolved to offer his services to the new Bishop, perhaps feeling that such a mission would give more purpose and direction to his life. In the final pages of "My Bee Book," he showed his great respect and affection for the Bishop and his eagerness to accompany him to New Zealand. He wrote: "I thank God he has permitted me to go with him. I pray to Him that my spirit may daily become more and

William Charles Cotton MA
1813 - 1879
Priest, Missionary and Bee Master

The Parish Church of St. John the Baptist, Windsor.
(Photograph courtesy of Judges of Hastings, www.judges.co.uk)

more like his - that He will bless us in the fulfillment of this prediction in His own good time."[13] But when William Cotton heard that his son had agreed to accompany Selwyn, he was not so pleased. In fact the decision incensed his father and caused him to write some harsh words to Windsor. "Selwyn has no right to lay his commands on you" he declared. "Does the Vow (of Ordination) that is on you, impose the duty of going to New Zealand? I think not."[14] When his son persisted with the plan, his father made it perfectly clear that he went without his sanction, and that he was to prove himself within four years and then return home. He summed up his attitude with the blunt statement "You are not missionary material."

Who was this man whom Cotton had decided to serve in New Zealand, contrary to his father's wishes?

William Charles Cotton MA
1813 - 1879
Priest, Missionary and Bee Master

George Augustus Selwyn

Born at Church Row, Hampstead, on April 5th 1809, Selwyn like Cotton, attended Eton College. It is said that he was "the best boy on the river, and nearly the first boy in learning." Besides being a good swimmer, he also excelled in diving. Many years later, in 1859, when he was 50 years old, his Melanesian mission ship ran aground. When it was re-floated it was necessary to examine the keel. Selwyn, dressed in tweed trousers and jersey, dived under the ship a number of times to discover how much damage had been done - a feat which earned him a salute of eleven guns from a French ship whose captain, with some of his officers, had looked on with admiration.

George Augustus Selwyn - the first AnglicanBishop of New Zealand.

Samuel Cousins A.R.A. after George Richmond.

Engraving.

By kind permission of the Hocken Collections, Uare Taoka o Hakena, University of Otago, Dunedin, New Zealand.

Selwyn, who went up to Cambridge in 1827, was a Scholar and afterwards a Fellow of St John's College. He rowed at seven for Cambridge in the first university boat race. To maintain his prowess as a swimmer he swam every day - whatever the weather. After taking his degree in classics and mathematics, he went back to Eton as a private tutor. Once again he spent much of his leisure on the river and in taking long country walks. After a time he decided to enter the ministry. In due course he was ordained and became a curate at Windsor Parish Church. Within a short space of time his energy and enthusiasm, combined with his deep religious faith and great personal charm began to transform the social and spiritual life of the parish.

In June 1839 he married Sarah Harriet, daughter of Sir John Richardson, a judge in the Court of Common Pleas. From the start she proved herself to be a loving and gracious wife, who, when the time came, faced the prospect of years of living in primitive conditions with equanimity and understanding.

Selwyn's Appointment

Such was his outstanding ability that, in 1841 at the age of 32, and though still only a curate, Selwyn was appointed to be the first Bishop of New Zealand. The salary was £1200-00 per annum - half of which was paid by the Church Missionary Society and half by the government. "The funny thing was," said Mrs Selwyn, "we could find so little to throw any light upon our future home. It seemed as far off as it well could be; it was just beginning to be colonized - the natives were wild and warlike."

George Augustus Selwyn was consecrated bishop by the Archbishop of Canterbury and the Bishops of London, Lincoln and Barbados in the Chapel of Lambeth Palace on Sunday October 17th 1841. On the last day of October, Bishop Selwyn, amid much sorrow, preached his farewell sermon in Windsor Parish Church. He took as his text Isaiah IX. 5 "The abundance of the sea shall be converted unto thee, the forces also of the Gentiles shall come unto thee." In the evening there was a final gathering of family and friends in the home of Reverend Edward Coleridge at Eton. On 20th December Selwyn, with his wife, Sarah, and their two year old son, William, travelled down to Plymouth to join the barque, *Tomatin*.

Mrs Selwyn, in her *"Reminiscences"*, explains how Cotton had unexpectedly announced his intention to join the Bishop's party and accepted the position of chaplain. She makes the following comment on his character: "while his love for the Bishop, his enthusiasm, his goodness and good nature and his cleverness would have made him a valuable helper, it was all largely balanced by a want of ballast which made one afraid of what he would do next. It was owing, poor fellow, to a temperament subject to alterations of the highest and lowest spirits, each phase lasting for some time. The news of our going found him in the depths after a year's work at Windsor."[15]

Mrs Selwyn goes on to say that, though Cotton gave her some anxious moments, he was full of enthusiasm for the mission, always helpful and showed great kindness and cheerfulness. She wrote: "Immediately he shot up into exuberance full of zeal and self devotion and thoroughly delighting in the prospect. How kind he ever was to me I cannot say, in how good a spirit he would take away any check I ventured to offer or how earnestly he desired to help the work in hand in his own eccentric way but he was an anxiety from time to time truly, also a great help from his cheeriness and life."[16]

Selwyn had an eye to the contribution that the twenty nine year-old Cotton could make to the success of the mission both as a Classical scholar and potential tutor, and for his practical skills. For instance his father had taught him to use various tools, including a lathe, which could be useful in what would almost certainly turn out to be a pioneering way of life. Also he had gained some knowledge of church construction from his father and he could ride a horse and row or sail a boat with some expertise.

William Charles Cotton MA
1813 - 1879
Priest, Missionary and Bee Master

The next two months were filled with the many preparations for the voyage. Whilst Selwyn was busy anticipating the needs of his colleagues and buying the necessary supplies and equipment, Cotton decided that he, too, would purchase some items for the Bishop's party. Unfortunately his inclination to overspend showed itself again. In a letter written on 3rd December 1841, Selwyn complained of Cotton's extravagance. He wrote: "But your unnecessary and lavish expenditure on your outfit, naturally alarms me, as it does your father." The Bishop went on to tell WCC that he had had to restrict his own spending to provide for the party, and Cotton should do the same. Selwyn objected to him buying things for which "there will not be house room and will finish up rotting on the beach." Also he objected to Cotton's proposal to provide a large printing press when the CMS had one ready to send out. He begged WCC not to order anything for general use and asked him to keep to his own responsibility. As the Librarian,[17] Selwyn made clear, this entailed looking after the shipment of books for the "Cathedral library," completing the Catalogue and studying the native language with a view to starting work on a translation of the Bible. As there was no further mention of this matter, presumably Cotton took note of the Bishop's pleas and exercised more restraint in his spending for the voyage.

After Selwyn's farewell sermon at Windsor, the party left for Plymouth and, late in December 1841, they set sail in the *Tomatin*. On board, besides the twenty three members of the Bishop's party and their luggage, were various animals, as well as four stocks of bees in their specially constructed hives.

William Charles Cotton MA
1813 - 1879
Priest, Missionary and Bee Master

Cotton's Plans for the Voyage

In the last chapter of "My Bee Book," which was published in 1842 after he had set sail, Cotton gave a detailed description of his scheme to transport several hives of bees to New Zealand. He explained that he hoped to leave England in the middle of winter, when his bees would be in a dormant state. To maintain them in this condition, he intended to keep them at a low temperature, well hidden and in a dry atmosphere. To achieve this he would place the hives in specially adapted hogsheads (large barrels) lined with thick felt. The bottom half of each barrel would be packed with ice to keep the bees at a cold temperature as the weather outside became warmer. As the ice melted, the water would be drained off through a tap at the foot of the barrel, as shown in the diagram below:

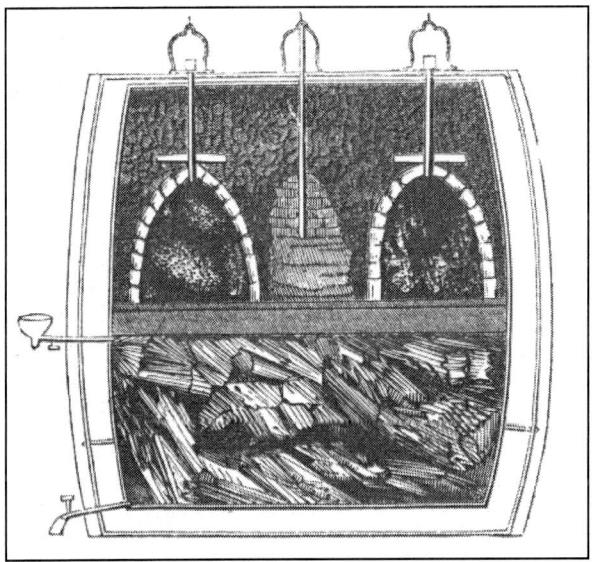

Cotton's drawing of how he intended to adapt a barrel to transport the bees. The hives can be seen suspended inside. "My Bee Book" page 392.

He then described the process by which he would remove the bees from their usual hives: "The bees will be moved from their bottom boards on some cold November day, and securely tied, each in a square cloth of dairy canvass." Next he explained how the hives would be placed over this and the top half of the barrel filled with cinders to exclude light and heat, and the bottom half packed with ice. By this means, Cotton wrote, "the bees will be put into a deep sleep; though I hope not an eternal one."[18] The evidence that Cotton carried out this plan and definitely took bees on board the *Tomatin* is contained in a letter to his sisters dated 30th December 1841, where he stated that every living thing on the ship was doing well, including his bees: "We are now becalmed for the first time since leaving Plymouth, and so, as our position will show you, have had a capital run. For five whole days we did not alter our tack............ All well, Mrs Selwyn, Bishop and Willie - dogs and Bees and self."

But what was the fate of these bees? Although some writers spoke of his "mastery over his favourites on shipboard," a contributor to the "Cottage Gardener and Country Gentleman" in December 1858 stated that the bees were thrown overboard because the sailors attributed the ship's stormy passage to the presence of the bees. Whether this is what actually happened, it is difficult to say. Certainly Cotton makes no mention of any such incident in his journal and, in any case, there were very few "stormy" days during the voyage. In fact, from the time of his embarkation at Plymouth until his arrival in Sydney, there is no reference in the Journal to his bees. However it would appear that some disaster must have befallen these hives because he spent the first part of his stay in New Zealand without any bees. In a letter written on 21st April 1843, nearly a year after his arrival, he stated that he hoped to have some bees sent over from friends in Sydney. He wrote as follows:

"My dear Arthur, my brother and my Godson...............
I hope this winter which is now coming to have some bees sent over to me from friends at Sydney, where they prosper, as I wrote to you

before, most wonderfully...... The mignonette which was sent to me last year grew capitally, but does not seed, as there are no bees - indeed this seems the fate of most English seeds."

Despite his apparent failure to transport bees successfully from England, as we shall see, Cotton worked hard to encourage bee keeping during his time in New Zealand, especially during the latter part of his stay.[1]

*This drawing appears on the last page of "My Bee Book."
Could it be a picture of the stern of the Tomatin?*

NOTES AND REFERENCES - CHAPTER ONE

[1] Letter from his father 1826 - Ms Acland, Bodleian Library.

[2] J B Atlay "Sir Henry Wentworth Acland - A Memoir" page 114.

[3] Letter from his father dated 13th February 1837.

[4] Ibid dated 18th April 1837.

[5] James F Robinson "British Bee Farming - Its Profits and Pleasures" 1889 page 105.

[6] Preface to "My Bee Book" page xl.

[7] "My Bee Book" page 275-277

[8] Letter from his father 18th April 1839 - Ms Acland, Bodleian Library.

[9] Ibid 27th May 1839.

[10] Letter from his father 27th May 1839.

[11] Ibid - 19th August 1839.

[12] Letter from his father 13th March 1840.

[13] "My Bee Book" page 397.

[14] Letter from his father September 1841.

[15] Sarah Selwyn "Reminiscences" page 15.

[16] Ibid page 15.

[17] In his list of the *Tomatin's* passengers at the start of his Journal, Cotton describes himself as "Librarian." However at other times he is referred to as the Bishop's chaplain. Perhaps both titles were equally applicable.

[18] "My Bee Book" 1842 page 394.

[19] For a detailed description of Cotton's bee-keeping exploits in New Zealand, the reader should consult Peter Barrett's book "William Charles Cotton - Grand Bee Master of New Zealand 1842 to 1847" published in 1997.

CHAPTER TWO

THE VOYAGE TO NEW ZEALAND

Setting Sail

In mid December 1841 the *Tomatin* set out from London but met with contrary winds in the Channel and had to return to port. The Bishop's party, which was to embark at Plymouth, had to wait twelve days for the ship to arrive. Of the friends who had come to see the Selwyns off, only one, the Reverend Edward Coleridge, was able to stay until the *Tomatin* finally sailed on Sunday 26th December (St Stephen's Day) 1841.

One can readily imagine the busy, often chaotic scene on board ship as the passengers prepared for departure, with their baggage and other belongings being hurriedly carried through to the cabins. Furthermore one can sense their excitement at the prospect of starting out on such a long voyage, but at the same time appreciate their sadness at leaving family and friends behind. This is how Mrs Selwyn described the situation:

"The Admiral on the Station kindly sent his barge to take us on board, where, after a crowded gathering for prayer in our cabin, the friends who came with us took their leave, and left us to our strongly-stirred feelings, and the hubbub of departure..

William Charles Cotton MA
1813 - 1879
Priest, Missionary and Bee Master

"A Parting Cheer." Reverend Coleridge and friends returning to the shore as the Tomatin prepares to leave Plymouth harbour.
A pencil sketch, probably by Caroline Palmer. By kind permission of the Master, Fellows and Scholars of Selwyn College, Cambridge.

The arrival of stores, the hoisting up of a side of beef and a sack of cabbage, then a belated passenger, and people rushing about clamouring for missing boxes, all this was, perhaps fortunately, not in harmony with deep feelings - so to our cabin to reduce chaos and to get things straight while we were yet alive and well."[1]

So after prayers for a safe passage and farewells from friends "who did not expect to see each other again in this world," the *Tomatin* sailed at 1-30pm precisely. The Bishop stood on the poop with his hat in his hand, whilst the Reverend Edward Coleridge who was returning to the shore in the dinghy, gave vent to his feelings by standing up and shouting **"God bless you! Floreat Ecclesia! Floreat Etona."** As the ship moved further and further away from the harbour, the Bishop and his party must have felt very emotional knowing that their mission would last several years. Soon, with a fair wind, the vessel passed the breakwater and by evening they had lost sight of land.

William Charles Cotton MA
1813 - 1879
Priest, Missionary and Bee Master

The *Tomatin,* a three masted barque, had been built at Greenock on the River Clyde in 1839. This was her second voyage to Australia. (See Appendix I) The captain, George McPherson, had a crew of fourteen men under his command. On board were the Bishop, Mrs Selwyn and their infant son, William, and accompanying them, Mary Martin, the wife of William Martin, the Chief Justice of New Zealand. The Bishop's party consisted of the following gentlemen: Reverend Thomas Whytehead, chaplain, Reverend W C Cotton, librarian. Two members of the Church Missionary Society - Reverend William Dudley and Reverend Charles Reay, respectively graduates of Oxford and Cambridge. The Reverend Robert Cole, an SPG[2] missionary whose special task would be to work among the European settlers. Also there were four students for Holy Orders: Mr Leslie, to be ordained for Norfolk Island, Henry Butt, a physician, William Evans, a former drawing master at Eton and William Nihill. Frederic Fisher and William Lowther were described as scholars. Other members of the party were Messrs Lisle, Watson, Farmer and Gott. Finally in this group were William Bambridge, catechist and schoolmaster, and his wife, Sophie.

A more unusual passenger was George Rupai, a Maori boy, who had been taken to England and sent to school in Battersea, and was now returning home. Very soon Selwyn enlisted his services to help him, and other members of the party, learn Maori. In addition there were six servants from the Bishop's household[3] and one, Robert Hussey, who was described as "a servant under Mr Cotton's care." In total, including the "Intermediates" (steerage passengers), there were fifty-two people on board.

How did they feel as they faced the terrible hazards of crossing sixteen thousand miles of ocean in a small sailing ship? Without a doubt their trust in God and their strong sense of comradeship would help to calm their fears. Also perhaps they felt some comfort in the knowledge that the *Tomatin* had already completed one voyage to Australia. However, in spite of these reassuring factors, they probably all had some qualms about their safety. They would be well aware of how, in the past, many ships had been caught in gales and foundered on some rocky coast. So everyone must have prayed earnestly for his or her safe deliverance.

William Charles Cotton MA
1813 - 1879
Priest, Missionary and Bee Master

Seasickness

After giving some information about the passengers and crew, Cotton stated he had made "a little leeway" for himself before he started his Journal so that he could have a taste of life at sea. However there seems to have been little time for that as seasickness took an immediate toll on him. By the first evening, he wrote: "I felt very queer and gradually grew sick about 4 o'clock. Nihill lent me a light. Sick two or three times in the course of the evening." He lay in his cabin all night with his clothes on, had no sleep and felt horribly sickly. The entry for the Monday 27th December reads: "Got up in the same clothes. All over the place. No wash...... rolled about on deck. Sick two or three times.... would not care if I had been killed. Felt Pea Green." According to a later letter, this was the only time during the voyage that he suffered from seasickness. The next day there were strong winds which, he wrote, "Carried away our Gaff but as, the wind was nearly aft, it did not hinder our run."

Two days later he was still feeling sickly, and some unsympathetic person told him that this was nothing to what was to come. At this point he related how he took "a bason (sic) of arrow root, drank every drop of it and felt very uncomfortable but did not, however, bring it up." On Friday 31st December he recorded how he lay in bed all day. For five days the *Tomatin* had sped down the English Channel and across the Bay of Biscay at between five and seven and a half knots, but on New Year's Day the ship was becalmed for the first time.

Owing to seasickness amongst the passengers many meals were missed in the first few days of the voyage. That evening (1st January 1842) eighteen members of the Bishop's party sat down to dinner - the largest number to date. Cotton recorded that on this day he had a drink of tea at breakfast and some cold boiled mutton for dinner. Afterwards he had a wash in one and a half pints of yellow-looking water and then passed the evening "pretty snugly."

William Bambridge recorded how, in order to meet the Bishop's requirements, the Captain had ordered the quarterdeck to be cleared and washed down. At 10 o'clock on Sunday 2nd January all hands were busy preparing for divine service - stowing away working materials, laying down carpets and arranging chairs for steerage passengers as well as for the Bishop and his party. By this time Cotton had recovered and was able to take part in the first service of the voyage.

The Bishop's Strict Regime

By Monday 3rd January nearly everyone else was suffering from seasickness and by the middle of the week few of the party were coming to dinner. However that morning the Bishop set all hands to work on the principle, says Cotton, of the schoolmaster to whom a boy complained of a bad headache. "Headache!" said the master, "there is nothing better than Greek grammar to cure a headache - so learn a double lesson this morning." The cure was very effective and "Lingua Novo Zealandica" (Maori) was found to be a capital substitute for Greek - "though," he says "there was no birch pickle to season it with."

Thus on board the *Tomatin* no one was allowed to be idle. Bishop Selwyn had given everyone ten days for seasickness and convalescence, and then all the party followed a strict programme: daily prayers at 8 o'clock, breakfast at 9 o'clock, then psalms and lessons in their original languages each at their appointed hour. Dinner was served at 4pm and tea at 7-30pm.
During the day there were also classes in mathematics and navigation which alternated with talks on New Zealand and the study of native languages - Maori, Tahitian and Rarotongan.[4] There is no doubt that learning Maori was given the highest priority in their daily programme. Mary Martin stated many years later that both her husband and the Bishop had always stressed that the Maori were to be "cared for and worked for." Selwyn maintained this programme of instruction, except for a few days, throughout the whole of their five-month voyage. As

Allan Davidson points out, this learning scheme might well have formed the "model for the studies to be pursued in a Church Missionary College."⁵

Mrs Selwyn wrote later:
"George kept his party hard at work learning Maori, he himself sticking to it the whole day. There was nothing to help him but an early, old and imperfect translation of St Matthew, and a Maori boy brought by some gentleman to England and whom we were taking back. He was of no use excepting for the pronunciation........... I am afraid that none of his pupils were half as diligent as he."⁶

By April 1842 Selwyn could speak Maori sufficiently well to converse with Rupai and catechize him in his own language. In fact the Bishop had learnt the native tongue so thoroughly that not only was he able to preach in Maori on the first Sunday after his arrival in New Zealand, but the natives wanted to know how many years he had lived in the country. Mrs Selwyn continues: "On board he got up a lesson ahead of us and we sat like good children round the table for two or three hours every morning learning it, the Maori boy supplying his part with the pronunciation."⁷

Mary Martin describes Rupai "as a walking dictionary" and maybe some of the Bishop's party gained by the opportunity to talk with him and practise their knowledge of Maori. However she did not think very highly of him. "He was not a favourable specimen for he had been the plaything of the servants' hall in holiday time, and had little more than superficial civilization. He left off English habits, with his English clothes on landing, and never sought for instruction or Christian teaching."⁸

Some years later Lady Martin made these comments about life on board the *Tomatin*:
"We had none of the modern luxuries required in steamers - no fresh bread, no stewardess to wait on us, no delicate fare........... If we had

plain living, we certainly had the opportunity of high thinking. Our party consisted of the Bishop of New Zealand, his two chaplains - both men of great gifts - and other clergymen and students. Daily classes for all who wished to learn the Maori language. No printed grammar, only a manuscript grammar and vocabulary. Had a walking dictionary in a Maori boy (Rupai) who was very useful and helped to teach correct pronunciation."[9]

On Tuesday 4th January William Bambridge noted "Porpoise around us and a few grampuses or small whales spouting about the vessel. They are either very pleased or very angry at the Ecclesiastical Freight which has ventured into their territories."[10]

Despite some adverse winds and rough seas, it appears that the *Tomatin* made good progress. Mrs Selwyn stated that the crew did not have to reef the topsails for seventy days.

A Schooner and a Brig

By Friday 7th January the island of Madeira, which lies 380 miles west of Morocco, was just visible in the distance. At sunrise a strong light could be seen playing on its hills. On the following Sunday the Bishop preached at divine service, whilst Mr Dudley read the lessons and Mr Whytehead presided. The next day they saw a rakish looking schooner a long way to leeward. Some people on board feared it might be a pirate ship. Later in the day a large brig appeared on the horizon and gradually drew closer. Eventually it was WCC who, with the aid of his large telescope, identified her as the *Retrench* from Greenock. Subsequently they found out she was sailing to Sierra Leone on the coast of West Africa. In the evening the wind abated so the Captain's gig was lowered. Cotton was chosen as one of the crew and they rowed over to the brig. Later he described how they were received on board "most civilly" and were given "capital meat and beautiful cold water." At Sierra Leone they were told the brig would be taking on "free" negroes for Demerrara, a small town in Guyana in the West Indies. As slave trading had been abolished in the British Empire in

William Charles Cotton MA
1813 - 1879
Priest, Missionary and Bee Master

1807, these men were almost certainly indentured labourers who were about to be shipped across the Atlantic. Cotton recorded how the deck had been cleaned "fore and aft" so that the ship could carry as many negroes as possible. Though these people were no longer kept in shackles, one wonders just how much conditions on these ships had improved since the days of slave trading.

Daily Life on Board

Below is Cotton's description of how he spent his day on the *Tomatin*:

"At 4 o'clock, or soon after, I turn out for morning watch. Then I have a showerbath. Daybreak very fine, though I miss the long days of old England very much - here in the Tropics (4th February) the sun does not rise long before 6.
8 o'clock: Prayers in the Cuddy (the cabin or saloon).

9 o'clock: Breakfast. Often at this time, or a little later, the Bishop takes Lunars with the Captain when the moon is visible.

10 o'clock: New Zealand lecture (concerning the study of the Maori language) till 11am.

11-30am: Greek Testament lesson of the day.

12-30pm: Bread and cheese.

1 o'clock: The synagogue (Hebrew) meets for the Psalms and the first lesson. I am working on the New Zealand concordance so I read Hebrew by myself. (Cotton and his colleague, Charles Reay, were working on a translation into Maori of the principal words of the Bible arranged alphabetically, with their relevant text).

3 o'clock or soon after, dinner, a long affair - lasting nearly two hours. Mrs Martin and all the Invalids dine on the poop (the highest deck at

the stern of the ship) - the dinner hoisted through the skylight on a swing table.

5 o'clock: All hands assemble on the poop. The Bishop reads Arabian nights or from Lockhart's ballads etc.

7-30pm: Tea.

10 o'clock: The ladies turn in, then the bathing tub comes into operation again and I soon turn in for the night.

WCC concluded his list of the day's events with the comment:
"It is really marvellous how this treadmill, and yet not useless life, makes the feathers grow on old Father Time's wing."[11]

Livestock

Something perhaps not always appreciated is that sailing ships in those days often had livestock on board to provide fresh food for the crew and passengers on long voyages. On the *Tomatin* there were a number of sheep, pigs, geese, cocks and hens, and at least one cow. It may have been the intention to add some of these animals, if they survived, to the livestock at the mission station in New Zealand.

By mid January the sheep needed shearing and the Bishop gave a hand by taking a pair of scissors and clipping one of them. Seeing Selwyn hard at work, Cotton remarked that he looked quite the patriarch in his episcopal dress. Shortly afterwards an incident occurred with one of the geese which suddenly jumped on to the ship's rail and flew into the sea. "Goosey, loosey," as Cotton called the event, was soon brought to a rapid conclusion. As the wayward goose refused all efforts to induce it to return, the ship's boat was lowered and one of the crew struck it with an oar. Needless to say it was then quickly retrieved for the dining table.

About a week later two pigs disgraced themselves. As they were unwell they had been allowed to wander about the deck. Cotton returned one afternoon to find they had gone into his cabin and made a mess. In his anger he kicked one out of the door and threw the other out of the porthole! In justification for this drastic action, he explained that the second pig was too small and sickly for the dining table and that drowning it was a merciful relief to all concerned.

The ship's company also supplemented their intake of fresh food by fishing, usually with hand lines cast out from the stern. They caught mostly bonito and albacore - these latter fish weighing about nine pounds on average. One day Rupai found a small shark on the end of a line that had been given to him. On Friday 21st January they caught their first dolphin. Cotton described it as a beautiful mammal, about a yard in length and that, in the water, it looked sky blue with gold-coloured fins.

As the voyage progressed daily prayers continued to be held in the cuddy at 8 o'clock in the morning. The Bishop was frequently to be seen among the sailors, talking to them and giving advice. Soon after their departure from Plymouth he had distributed a great many Prayer Books and Bibles among them. Cotton saw him one day in his full Bishop's dress during divine service sharing his hymn book with one of the crew. The sailors, as might be expected, did not attend Church as regularly as the Bishop would have liked.

A day or two before they reached the Equator, they had a close encounter with the *Vixen*. The two ships approached each other to exchange mail but unfortunately, either through poor navigation or a sudden gust of wind, the vessels scraped alongside each other. When Cotton came on deck he found everyone crouching down under the bulwarks to avoid the spars that they thought might come crashing down upon them. He wrote afterwards: "thank God she scraped away and fell astern, carrying away only our lower studding sail boom, and leaving some of her sail in our rigging."

William Charles Cotton MA
1813 - 1879
Priest, Missionary and Bee Master

When a little later the Bishop joined the boarding party, Cotton thought at first he went out of curiosity, but then realized it was probably to help assuage any ill feelings between the two contending Captains. Despite the accident this was the first opportunity for those on board to send letters home.

On Wednesday 26th January they celebrated crossing the line. First they had tea on the poop deck. Afterwards Chips, the carpenter, appeared wearing an old macintosh. He paraded up and down the deck, impersonating Neptune, much to everyone's amusement. During the revelry several party games were played and there was much good-humoured banter.

A few days later, on Sunday 30th January, they were celebrating Cotton's twenty-ninth birthday which made him feel somewhat homesick. Later he noted: "Thought of all home friends, I even lacked letters on my breakfast table." That same day it was his turn to preach at divine service. Rather aptly he chose the theme "They that go down to the sea in ships and do business in great waters." He declared that the Bishop liked his sermon and came to his cabin afterwards and spoke very kindly about it.

During the evening of Friday 4th February he and his friend, William Evans, enjoyed a novel experience. They were allowed to climb the main rigging for the first time. They found the view, the breeze and rolling motion of the ship most delightful and felt quite safe when perched on the top most cross tree. Cotton recorded later that since this first venture he had spent many pleasant evenings aloft and, from that commanding height, he had enjoyed several fine sunsets, played some good games of chess and had written many verses.

One day the sight of a school of flying fish caused great excitement on board. Suddenly between fifty and a hundred of them rose up in the air above the waves. Cotton stated that they flew much more swiftly and much farther than he had expected. Some travelled nearly two hundred yards, rising "just over the crest of a wave, skimming so close to it that their fins were moistened by the water......" The sight of these amazing fish inspired him to write a poem about them. Below are the first two verses. The whole poem can be found in Appendix II.

The Flying Fish

As oe'r th'Atlantic wave was cast
    The first glad beams of day
Amazed I saw a fairy form
    Glance swift from out the spray

All silver were its glittering scales
    Its wings all black as night
Half fish half bird it seemed to mock
    The swallow in its flight

Managing the Stores

By the third week of February the Captain decided not to put in to Cape Colony, South Africa, but to press on with the voyage. As a result it became necessary to economize on stores. Water consumption per person was reduced to a maximum of five pints a day. With the Captain's consent the Bishop undertook to manage the stores so as to make the stock hold out.

Cotton complained that some of the steerage passengers had tremendous appetites and usually gave them full play, much to the Bishop's disgust. With the number of livestock on board rapidly diminishing, each person was allowed only one helping of fresh meat per day but could fill up on salt beef and rice. By making use of the ducks and by opening individual cases of preserved meat, Selwyn managed to arrange some tit-bits for the ladies. Apparently the ducks and geese on board had thrived but the poultry had died, probably because of the rigours of the voyage.

William Charles Cotton MA
1813 - 1879
Priest, Missionary and Bee Master

A Piece of Good Fortune

Tuesday 22nd February turned into a pleasant, calm evening so the boat was lowered. The Bishop joined the party but, Cotton declared, it was "like going to sea in a sieve as the water streamed in through every seam." The boat had been hanging on the davits since they crossed the line. When they had gone some way ahead of the ship, Selwyn gave his consent for them to bathe, as the Captain had assured him he had never heard of sharks in such southerly waters. Cotton, Evans and Farmer had a "glorious plunge," but they soon climbed back in the boat as the ship drew alongside them very rapidly.

That same evening, just as it was getting dark, a large shark could be seen circling the ship. It took a fancy to the salt pork which some of the crew had suspended from the bows to wash out the brine. The sailors taunted the creature by drawing up the meat whenever it came near. Cotton declared it gave him quite a turn to think that the Captain's assertion that there were no sharks hereabouts had been plainly disproved. He wrote: "I, for one, was not a little thankful to feel both my legs safe in their places."

On Sunday 27th February, during divine service, a terrible howling noise could be heard. It turned out to be the dog, Blackie, who was sick and seemed to be having a fit. Cotton took him into his cabin, put on some thick gloves and managed to give him a dose of castor oil. By the next morning he was well on the way to making a good recovery, lapping up milk and later eating some meat from a freshly slaughtered pig.

Learning Maori

In his comments for 12th March, Cotton stated that, as usual, on a Saturday morning, they were repeating everything they had learned in Maori since their lessons started. He thought the number of New Zealand words that they were packing away in their heads was quite amazing. It is not surprising that the exercise took them one and a half hours. Evidently they were having some success in memorizing the Maori words as the Bishop was more pleased with their performance than he had been previously. WCC showed a wry sense of humour when he asked, "What will English ladies with delicate mouths think of "Turinginganga' which means 'married' or 'wakamaoritia'?

Rupai, the native boy, was still helping them with their lessons, especially with the pronunciation of words. The youngster had made everybody laugh when he told them that the Bishop had washed in "soda water" every morning since he came on board. Immediately they imagined the huge number of bottles he must have used and what an expense he had incurred. The explanation turned out to be that Rupai had made a mistake in the translation. The Bishop had been really washing everyday in salt water, not soda water!

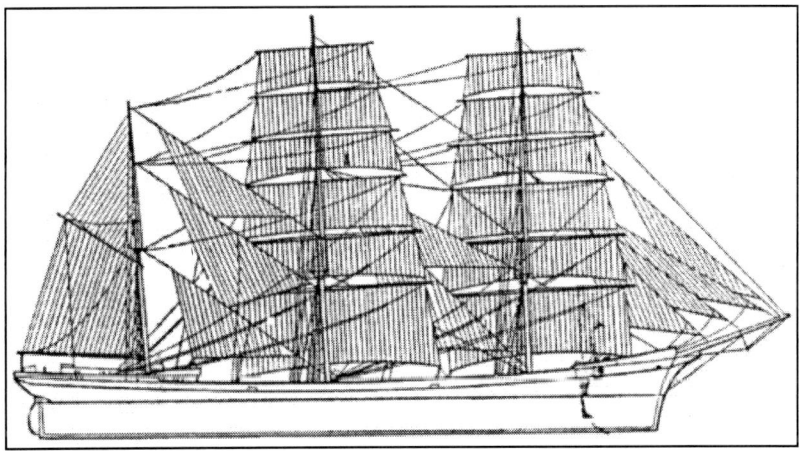

A typical three masted barque of the period.

William Charles Cotton MA
1813 - 1879
Priest, Missionary and Bee Master

Services on Board

From the start of the voyage, the Bishop's party held divine worship on a regular basis. Below and on the next page are diagrams based on those that appear in the Journal. They show the arrangements made for holding these services: the quarterdeck served as the Church, the poop as the Lady Chapel and between decks as the Crypt. WCC pointed out that the quarter or main deck was only used for this purpose on the first Sunday of the voyage and on Easter Day, as it was found to interfere with the working of the ship and the duties of the steward.

Church or Quarter Deck

1. Bishop's Seat
2. Mr. Whytehead (or other clergyman)
3. Seats for the clergy.
4. Seats for the ladies.
5. Crew and intermediate passengers.
6. Bishop's household.

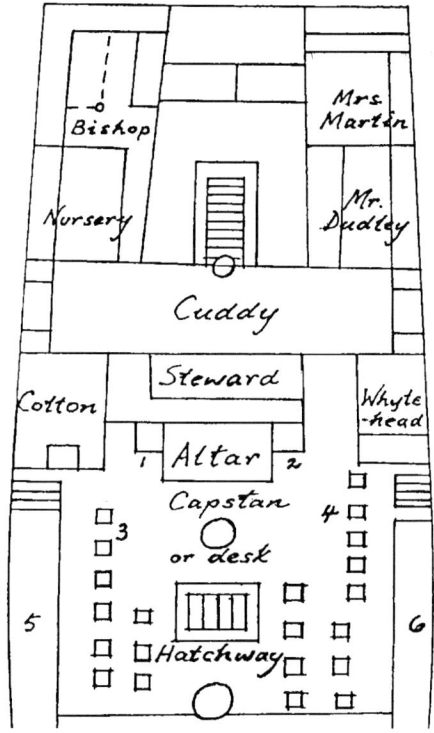

Arrangements for church services on the quarterdeck.
Journal Volume I.

William Charles Cotton MA
1813 - 1879
Priest, Missionary and Bee Master

He stated that when the between decks was used as a crypt, the Bishop sat at point d, and the other parson at point e. Our party, he wrote, were in all the cabins, like sleeping buoys. The passengers were in the sections marked f. Selwyn covered the long table with his plaids, and the medicine chest, with his Windsor plain table cover. The servants sat round at b - by the mizzen. Finally, he added, "every man buys his own candles."

Poop or Lady Chapel   **Crypt Between Decks**

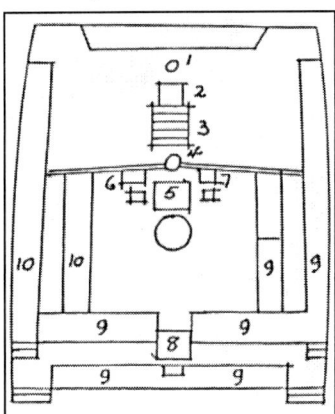
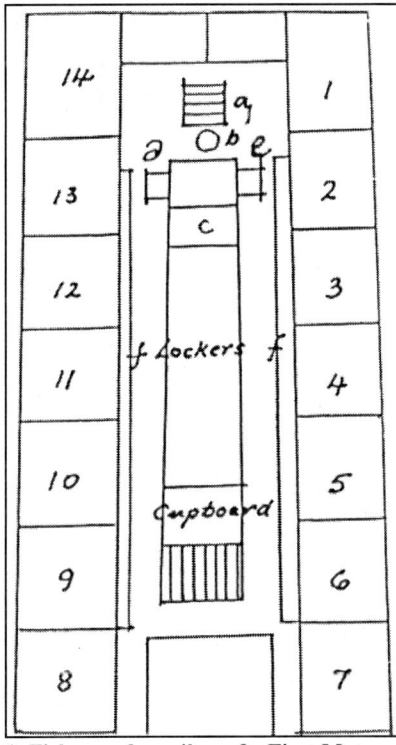

1. Wheel
2. Binnacle
3. Hale buoy
4. Mizzen mast
5. Altar
6. Bishop
7. Whytehead
8. Reading desk and pulpit made of ship's filter.
9. Seats for Clergy and our party.
10. Intermediates and sailors' seats made of hencoops.

Arrangements for divine worship between decks

1. Fisher and pupil
2. Cole
3. Reay
4. Lowther
5. Bishop's servants
6. Evans
7. James and Francis
8. Mrs Watts and children
9. First Mate
10. Lisle
11. Bull
12. Bambridge
13. Watson
14. Packages

Divine worship between decks must have been a remarkable scene with the Bishop's party sitting in the cabins and the steerage passengers crowding in near the lockers. The Bishop at the head of the gangway conducting the service and his half-hidden listeners struggling to hear his words against the noise of the sea and the ship's rigging and all enveloped in darkness, except for the spots of light thrown up by the burning candles.

Crossing the Indian Ocean

At daybreak on Thursday 24th March they sighted the island of St Paul - the first land seen since they left the Western Islands. Cotton wrote that the island was volcanic, uninhabited and without trees, but covered with long coarse grass. There were several large lagoons with plenty of fish. Slowly the *Tomatin* edged her way southwards and before breakfast was over, St Paul had disappeared from sight.

In the evening such a strong breeze arose that the halyard and tack of the foretop studding sail broke. The sail was carried away so that a large hole appeared in the foretopsail obliging the crew to reef it. Rupai was soon, Cotton recorded, "aloft like a monkey tying the reef points and enjoying himself in a pelting storm."

Good Friday 25th March

Two services were held with the Bishop leading the prayers and Reverend Whytehead delivering the sermon. Both services took place in the Crypt because it was too cold on the deck. During the week the Bishop had been working hard to prepare some of the steerage passengers for confirmation on Easter Sunday. At the same time Reay and Dudley had talked with the sailors every night about their faith but Cotton called them "a hopeless set to deal with."

At breakfast each person received, what was grandly called, a large hot cross bun - in reality it was a big, highly spiced lump of dough - the best the cook could manage, as there were no eggs left, since the hens had perished weeks before.

William Charles Cotton MA
1813 - 1879
Priest, Missionary and Bee Master

On Easter Sunday there were about forty communicants, of whom eight or nine were steerage passengers. It was Cotton's turn to preach at the morning service. He was pleased when the Bishop came to his cabin afterwards and congratulated him on his sermon. The next day for the first time in weeks one of the sheep was killed. The sailors threw some offal overboard and almost at once, to everyone's delight, twelve albatross appeared at the stern and started diving into the water for the discarded meat. Normally there were no more than two or three of these birds around the ship at any one time. Later in the day a gentle breeze sprang up and the *Tomatin* bounded along at the rate of 7 to 8 knots.

A few days later the ship encountered one of its worst bouts of bad weather. The Captain gave the order to double reef the top sails as the vessel was labouring in heavy seas and shipping a great deal of water. As everyone half expected, it turned out to be a bad night - no one on board got much sleep. Many were absent at breakfast and very few attended the morning lecture. Those who were present found that the ship was making so much noise they could hardly hear the Bishop speak. The dead lights were down* and it was so bitterly cold that they were forced to keep the cuddy door shut. Cotton gave this verdict on the day: "we have had in this one day a taste of the discomfort which could have been ours had we had a bad, instead of a fair passage." Finally he made the curious remark that in the storm "the cow was rolled out of the long boat," which we can only assume meant that in bad weather she was tethered there for safety's sake.

* Strong shutters fixed inside or outside the portholes to keep water out during a storm.

William Charles Cotton MA
1813 - 1879
Priest, Missionary and Bee Master

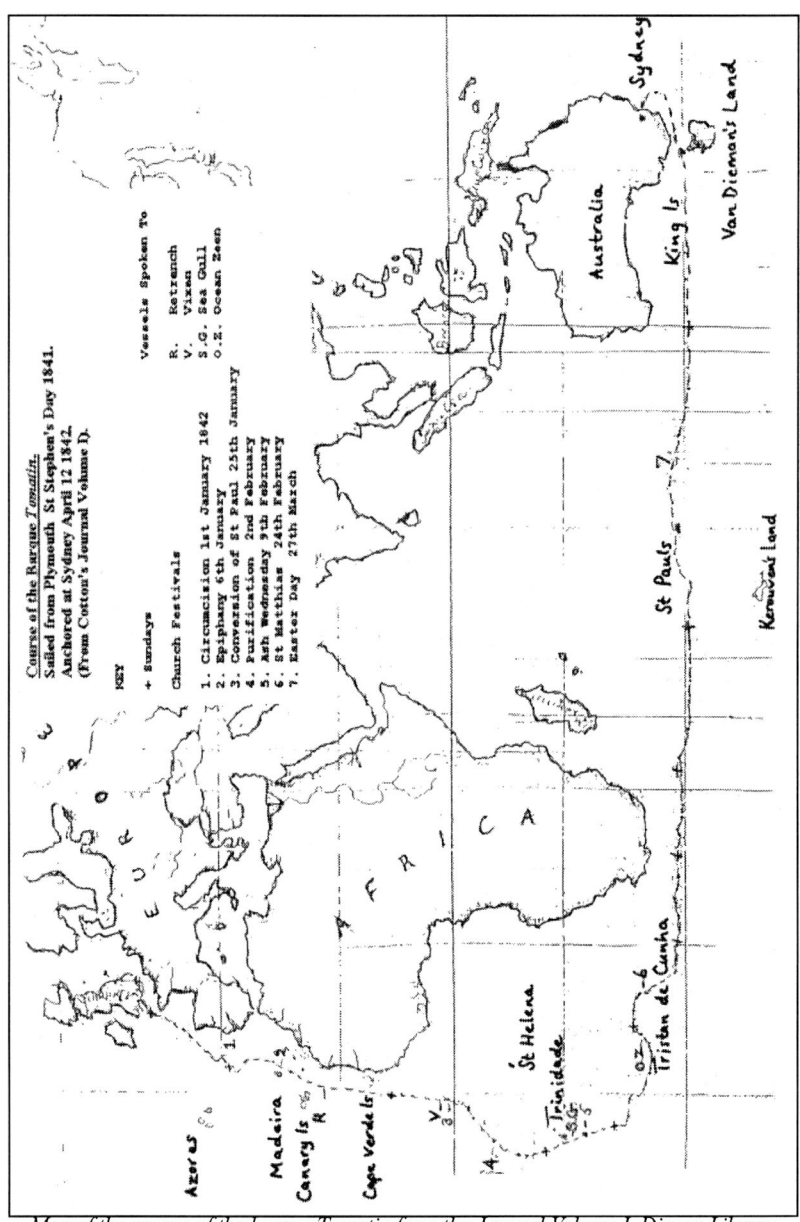

Map of the course of the barque Tomatin from the Journal Volume I. Dixson Library, State Library of New South Wales.

William Charles Cotton MA
1813 - 1879
Priest, Missionary and Bee Master

Lunar Observations and Good Morale

Despite his many other duties, Selwyn found time throughout the voyage to improve his navigational skills. He became expert at taking lunar observations and then working with Captain McPherson to calculate the position of the ship. "By the time we reach New Zealand," Cotton wrote, "I have no doubt the Bishop will be able to take command of this schooner should we ever be placed in that situation."

On Friday 8th April the Bishop and the Captain calculated that the ship was a degree more to the eastward than they had expected. As a result orders were given to keep a sharp look out for land, as soon they should be in sight of King Island at the entrance to the Bass Strait, off the coast of Australia. In the meantime, with the voyage progressing well, the Bishop's party was working harder than ever to master the Maori language. They were concentrating their minds, wrote Cotton, "like men the last week before they go up for their examination." Adding that, on the last leg of their journey between Sydney and New Zealand, they will be "perpetually in a state of repitition" (sic) - that is revising and testing themselves on their knowledge of the native tongue.

At breakfast the next morning the Captain spoke of the inevitable quarrels that break out in many ships on long voyages. He explained how tempers could become frayed with everyone living in cramped quarters, and often eating monotonous food, with little or no recreation and nothing to occupy their minds. And, if the ship is becalmed, how the intense heat can play upon people's minds, or in stormy seas how everyone can become depressed by the wet and the cold. But the *Tomatin* was an exception, he declared, because the Bishop and his party had a high moral purpose and everyone was kept busy and in good spirits.

William Charles Cotton MA
1813 - 1879
Priest, Missionary and Bee Master

Some aspects of life on board the ship are hard to imagine but here and there Cotton gives us an insight into how they spent their days. One such example is this plan of the seating arrangements of the Bishop's party at mealtimes shown below:

Seating arrangements in the ship's mess. Journal Volume I page 149. Dixson Library, State Library of New South Wales.

From his position at the end of the row, Cotton had a good view of the line of faces down the length of the table. "A fine Physiognomical study" he called it. "No two faces are alike. Red whiskers are in a great majority." What a picture his words conjure up! One can readily imagine the crowded mess with the Bishop, Mrs Selwyn, his chaplain and other colleagues sitting on benches huddled together at the table. All these earnest clergy and a handful of ladies chattering away at mealtimes, doing their best to forget their hardships and make the most of their often unappetizing diet. And, as frequently happens in these situations, feeling duty bound to always occupy the same places at the table. "After having stuck to our places for three months, there seems to be a sort of natural propriety in our positions, so that change would seem to violate the harmonies of Nature."

William Charles Cotton MA
1813 - 1879
Priest, Missionary and Bee Master

The Promise of Land

During the morning the Captain remarked that he knew the pigs smelt land by the way in which they ran about with their noses in the air. On the same morning Cotton noted that their stock of animals had reached "a wonderful uniformity - one sheep, one pig, one goose" - a statement that doesn't seem to tally with the Captain's remarks as to the number of pigs. With such a small amount of livestock left, perhaps it was just as well that they were getting near to Sydney, although they did have water for several weeks and salted provisions for six months.

The following morning, Monday 11th April, there was a brisk wind blowing and soon an immense number of birds were circling over the ship. The general opinion was that they were young albatross but Cotton thought they were rather squatter in shape and, therefore, some other species. With the expectation of seeing land at any time, all eyes were on the look out. At about 1-30pm a cry arose. They had made the first sighting of the Australian coast. It was Cape Otway about fifteen miles away. Later in the afternoon King Island could be seen. At this point the Bass Strait was about seven leagues wide and the ship was sailing in mid-channel. Cotton noted: "We have fallen in with the land at the right time of day so as to have a clear run all night towards Curtis Island which we expect to see tomorrow at sunrise."

As there would not be another Sunday at sea, the Bishop gave notice that a public service of thanksgiving would be held for their safe voyage on the evening before their arrival in Sydney. By five o'clock the next morning all the passengers were on deck. As the sun rose a most beautiful panorama met their eyes. First they saw the island of Rondondo, with its precipitous cliffs reaching down to the sea. Then they could make out the long line of the Australian coast stretching away to the north and, not far ahead, Wilson's Promontory, its southern most point. One can imagine the general sense of well being felt by the passengers and crew as the ship scudded through the Strait with the sun lighting up the hills beyond the distant coastline. The islands of Moneurs and Curtis appeared on the port and then, on the starboard, a long distance away, the Devil's Tower.

A Double Tragedy

On Tuesday 12th April 1842, as they were approaching Sydney Heads, their first and only disaster occurred - two sailors were tragically drowned.
As they were close to their destination, the Bishop had decided to hold the thanksgiving service on that evening. After dinner, whilst the Bishop put his finishing touches to his sermon in the cuddy, all hands came on to the poop. Cotton was sitting with Mrs Martin looking over a book when he heard a heavy splash and the cry "Man Overboard!" Despite their nearness to Sydney, the steerage passengers had been given their weekly allowance of stores and, unfortunately, they had passed a quantity of spirits to the crew. According to the Bishop, Thomas Brown had become intoxicated and as a result had fallen into the sea from the main yard arm. At the time the ship was travelling at some seven and a half knots, and they had gone a long way before a boat could be lowered. Though the men rowed hard to the spot where Brown was last seen, they were too late to save him.

On their return to the *Tomatin*, as the tackles were being hooked on, the ship rolled and the boat got swamped. As a result another man, Alexander Dick, was drowned. Fortunately the Bishop had the presence of mind to throw down an inflated life preserver and by this means Robert Watson, the second mate, was saved. Similarly another sailor, Riley, clung to an oar and he, too, was rescued.

Everyone on board was appalled by these sad events and a great gloom fell over the ship. A little later their thanksgiving became a solemn service in memory of the two men who had been drowned. A "sorrowful and mournful" occasion, wrote Cotton, and the only event that had marred the general good fortune of the voyage. In the evening Selwyn asked to see the two survivors. Cotton relates how the Bishop

William Charles Cotton MA
1813 - 1879
Priest, Missionary and Bee Master

"spoke to them very kindly and very solemnly, advising them to keep a yearly remembrance of the day." Then he gave a copy of the service, beautifully written out by Mr Bambridge, to each of them, together with a Prayer Book with the following inscription:

> Presented by
> The Bishop of New Zealand
> to
> Robert - Watson
> April 12th 1842
> as a memorial of his preservation
> from death by drowning on that day
> and of the death of two Seamen of
> the Barque "Tomatin"
> off the Coast of Australia.
> viz
> Tobias Branselans
> and
> Alexander Dick

The Bishop's message inscribed in copies of the funeral service given to the two survivors. Journal Volume I page 169. Dixson Library, State Library of New South Wales.

The day after this tragedy, towards evening, the weather took a turn for the worse. The following day, Wednesday 14th April, Cotton noted: "Late last night I went on deck and found it blowing harder than it has done since we left England. We were under double-reefed topsails, with a reef in the mainsail. The ship was rolling very much and the night very dark. At times there were furious squalls with occasional hailstorms. But we had cleared all the dangers of Bass Straits and I turned in with a perfect sense of security."

William Charles Cotton MA
1813 - 1879
Priest, Missionary and Bee Master

By noon the next day they were thirty-two miles south of Sydney and at dusk they could see the first windmill and the lighthouse on the south head of Sydney harbour. The next day, shortly after dawn, they ran through the Sydney Heads which were less than a mile apart and very rocky.

Soon a whaleboat appeared from a small creek to larboard (that is, port) bringing a pilot out to the ship. To everyone's surprise, they found that the four men rowing the boat were Maoris. Mrs Martin later described them as "tall, fine looking men, dressed in white duck trousers, jackets and straw hats."[12] Selwyn was elated at the sight of the natives, who by this time were lolling in their seats, as their boat was now undertow at the stern. Without hesitation he went over to speak to them. They were astonished to hear the Maori language, Cotton says, "coming from a mouth under a shovel hat." The Bishop's readiness to speak to them was strangely contrasted with Rupai's shyness. Rupai would not speak a word. "They don't know me" was all he would say.

A faint southerly breeze blew as they sailed across Sydney harbour. The coves and bays, with their tree-filled slopes down to the water's edge, could not fail to impress. Not surprisingly, Cotton described the scene as "excessively beautiful." One of the first things they saw of Sydney town was the spire of St Francis - the Bishop's Church, which WCC thought was very plain. As they were approaching their landing place, suddenly there was a heavy thump. By some mischance the pilot had allowed the ship to scrape on a rocky point, but fortunately they slid over the obstacle without too much damage. Shortly afterwards the welcome cry "Let go the anchor!" rang out. They had arrived in Sydney. The longest leg of their voyage had been successfully completed.

William Charles Cotton MA
1813 - 1879
Priest, Missionary and Bee Master

From Sydney to the Bay of Islands

As a result of this unfortunate accident, it was found that some of the copper sheets that protected the *Tomatin's* hull had been torn away. Inevitably this meant delaying the voyage to New Zealand as the repair would take several weeks. The disappointment felt by Selwyn and his party was to some extent countered by the hearty welcome given them by Bishop Broughton. The Bishop, Mrs Selwyn and Willie were invited to stay at the Bishop of Australia's house at Wooloomooloo, which Cotton described as "the fashionable Kensington of Sydney." The rest of the party was accommodated nearby, thanks to Mr Robert Campbell, the Church Missionary Society's agent. He kindly put a large, empty house (which he had just purchased) at their disposal. Cotton and his colleagues slept on the floor, four to a room, each person having a mattress and blanket. What the house lacked in comfort it made up for by its fine situation. It had the most beautiful views of the many coves of Sydney harbour. Cotton observed: "It is a most lovely situation, looking over at least five miles of Sydney Cove. It is like a succession of lakes, wooded down to the water's edge. The shores are rocky but not high."

Everyone seems to have enjoyed their time in Sydney, except that many of them suffered from mosquito bites, including young Willie, who Cotton says, looks "at present very like a pincushion." During their stay the Governor, Sir George Gipps, took them on a visit to Botany Bay, though they found it somewhat deserted as, some years before, it had ceased to be a convict settlement. Cotton called the expedition with the two bishops "an Episcopal Pic Nic." On another occasion they went up country into the Blue Mountains. The Governor sent the Bishops, Mrs Selwyn and one or two of their companions in his barge to Paramatia where he arranged for them to be taken by carriage to Penrith. On their return to Paramatia, they stayed overnight at Government House.

Whilst staying in Sydney, Cotton sent home to England a small deal box by the *Middlesex,* which set sail on 15th May. The box contained various items for his family, including the first volume of his journal, the outside of which had become soiled through constant use. In one of his letters he asked his sister, Phoebe, if she could use her sewing skills and make a cover for the next volume. Also he had put in the box "a bottle of Botany Bay honey for Teddy[13] not made by native but by English bees" and some bird skins for his mother. The latter, he wrote, were cheap (the birds were as common as sparrows) and had not meant any "improper extravagance" - a reference, no doubt, to his problem with overspending at Oxford.

One sad occurrence, which must have hung like a dark cloud over the Bishop's party, was the serious illness of the Reverend Thomas Whytehead. As an undergraduate at St John's College, Cambridge, he had shown great promise and gained his BA in 1837 and his MA in 1840. The following year, at the age of 26, he agreed to go with Selwyn as his chaplain. The Bishop's plan was that Whytehead would remain at the base and be head of the mission schools and eventually Master of the College. Unfortunately Whytehead, who had suffered from asthma since childhood, became gravely ill by the time they reached Sydney. Probably the damp conditions on board the *Tomatin* had aggravated his condition. Shortly after his arrival, an acute coughing spasm caused him to rupture a blood vessel. On medical advice he was forced to remain in Sydney when the rest of the party sailed for the Bay of Islands. Sadly consumptive symptoms were diagnosed and he was unable to complete the voyage until some months later.

A Change of Plan

After five weeks of waiting Mrs Martin, who was travelling out to New Zealand to join her husband, the Chief Justice, began to grow very impatient at the delay. One evening, Cotton wrote, they had "a Drama night." She decided to use her "woman's wit" and persuasive powers to convince Selwyn that a small number of them should complete the voyage in advance

William Charles Cotton MA
1813 - 1879
Priest, Missionary and Bee Master

of the rest. The Bishop eventually agreed that he and William Evans, along with Mrs Martin and Mrs Smith, would sail in a few days time. However Evans was on a visit up country and did not return in time, so Selwyn asked WCC to go in his place.

On Thursday 19th May they set sail in the *Bristolian*, a brig of 160 tons burden, commanded by Captain Thomas. They had a fast run and anchored in Auckland harbour on May 30th, 1842, - "a wet and dreary day." Mary Martin was overjoyed to see her husband again and as soon as possible they returned to their home in Taurarua. According to Mrs Martin it was "a long, one storied cottage.....perched upon a hill. There was hardly a shrub to be seen in those days."[14] Cotton explained that the house, which was nearly two miles from the town, had no road to it and "such a muddy path that it must be impassable all the winter to the petticoat-wearing species of the Genus Homo."[15]

Judge Martin and Attorney General Swainson had arrived in Auckland in October 1841. They had brought with them the parts of two prefabricated houses, which were set up on either side of a stream on the hillside above Taurarua Bay, or as the Aucklanders came to call it, Judges Bay. William Martin, a friend of Bishop Selwyn from their Cambridge days, and his fiancée, Mary, were married a few weeks before he left England.

They agreed that he should go on ahead to look after the construction of their new home. The young Mary Martin travelled out to New Zealand in the *Tomatin* a few months later. As Una Platts explains,[16] as things were guessed to be primitive in Auckland and Martin's fiancée very delicate, it had been thought best for him to come out alone; "so they were married and parted at the Church steps," as the Reverend FH Spencer put it, "he to go on board the ship to come to New Zealand, she to wait till he was settled."

William Charles Cotton MA
1813 - 1879
Priest, Missionary and Bee Master

William Martin, Chief Justice of New Zealand. J Dickson after J Carpenter. Auckland City Libraries. Engraving.

Mary Martin, who came out to New Zealand on the Tomatin to join her husband. Richmond Collection, Auckland, City Libraries.

Despite the inclement weather Selwyn and Cotton must have been excited to see the coast of New Zealand at long last and to sail into the beautiful Waitemata harbour. And then to have the great pleasure of meeting Capt Hobson RN, the first Governor of the colony, who had invited them to reside at Government House. During their stay they went on a number of expeditions, including a voyage to Rangitoto, an island off the Waitemata harbour, and to the Bay of Islands. On another occasion they accompanied Mr George Clarke, the Protector General of Aborigines, on a visit up the Thames Valley to see an old heathen chief called Teraia. The latter had recently attacked some Christian natives and indulged in a bout of cannibalism. Selwyn described their encounter with Teraia as follows:

William Charles Cotton MA
1813 - 1879
Priest, Missionary and Bee Master

"On Wednesday June 8th we walked twelve miles along the beach to the fortified village (pa) of Teraia, the leader of the massacre. On our way we passed several Christian villages, beautifully situated among shady trees at the foot of the wooded hills sloping down to the sea. ...... We observed everywhere on their cultivations the greatest abundance of provisions - potatoes, maize, kumers (sweet potato) and pumpkins, with pigs and fish in abundance. Teraia's Pa is strongly fortified, after the native manner with strong palisades........"[17]

After waiting some time they were invited to a korero with the chief who eventually agreed to surrender the slaves taken by him and to behave peaceably in the future. The visitors were no doubt relieved that such a wild and warlike chief had given them a civil reception and that he had agreed to most of their demands.

Government House, Auckland, showing the North Head of the Waitemata Harbour.
Edward Ashworth. Sepia wash. E-216-f-015.
Alexander Turnbull Library, Wellington, New Zealand

During their two weeks stay in Auckland, Cotton noted later, the Bishop had accomplished "an immensity of business." WCC seems to have greatly enjoyed the company of the Hobsons and their family. In a letter home, describing his only wants, he asked for "hats, clothes and a tin of ginger barley sugar for the little Hobson children." These days at Auckland, he declared, were the most pleasant he had spent since his journey began.

William Charles Cotton MA
1813 - 1879
Priest, Missionary and Bee Master

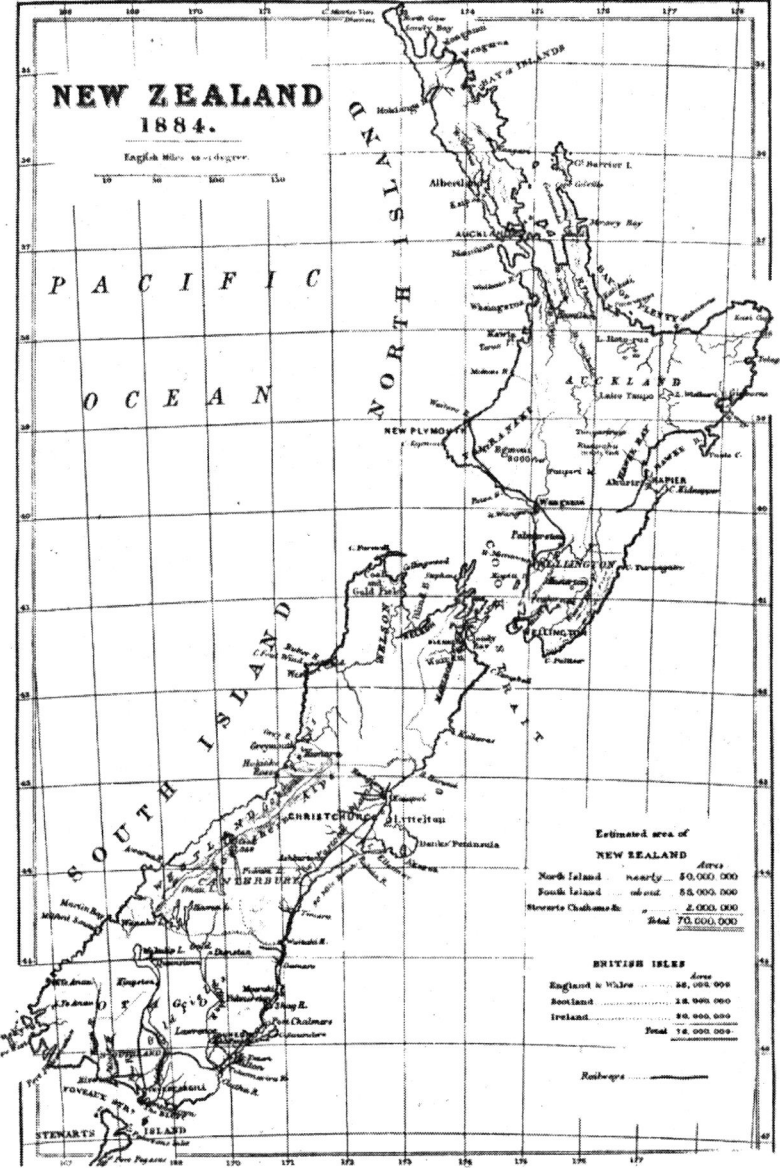

Map of New Zealand in the 19th century from Lady Martin's book "Our Maoris" 1884.

On 12th June they sailed for the Bay of Islands in the *Wave*, a small schooner of 60 tons. Unfortunately they had to endure a rough passage. They met with gale-force winds and high seas that obliged the Captain to treble reef the mainsail and to lay to for a couple of nights. Even worse, Selwyn became very ill. Cotton wrote that the Bishop had "a bad attack as well as being seasick." They were both very relieved when the vessel finally reached the Bay of Islands.

NOTES AND REFERENCES - CHAPTER TWO

[1] Sarah Selwyn "Reminiscences" page 16.

[2] The Society for the Propagation of the Gospel.

[3] The Bishop's servants were: Edward Arnold, Mrs Watts, Harriet Watts, William Watts, Ann Stapley and Mary Crump.

[4] Ruth Etherington "William Charles Cotton." Journal of the Auckland - Waikato Historical Societies August 1980 page 3.

[5] Allan K Davidson "Selwyn's Legacy" page 21.

[6] Sarah Selwyn "Reminiscences" page 16.

[7] Ibid page 16.

[8] Mary Martin "Our Maoris" page 2.

[9] Ibid page 3.

[10] William Bambridge Diaries.

[11] Journal Volume I page 12

[12] Mary Martin "Our Maoris" 1884 page 3.

[13] WCC's youngest brother, Joseph Edward.

[14] Marry Martin "Our Maoris" 1884 page 4

[15] Journal Volume I

[16] Una Platts "The Lively Capital" page 101.

[17] GH Curteis "Bishop Selwyn of New Zealand and Lichfield" page 47.

CHAPTER THREE

THE WAIMATE MISSION STATION

Bishop Selwyn's New Headquarters

Bishop Selwyn and Reverend Cotton had finally reached the Bay of Islands on Monday 20th June 1842, but the *Wave* had become becalmed just inside the heads off Cape Brett sixteen miles from Paihia. In spite of feeling unwell and suffering from seasickness, Selwyn decided to complete the voyage in his own boat, with Cotton and Rupai manning the oars. Archdeacon Henry Williams of the Church Missionary Society, who was waiting to greet them, said later how he had been impressed by the sight of their new Bishop drawing up his boat on to the beach. He added that he felt it was a good indication of Selwyn's suitability for his new position.

They spent five days at Paihia, two of them visiting the Waimate, where they were able to make some preparations for the arrival of Mrs Selwyn and the rest of the party. Just as they had completed their business and returned to the coast, "the *Tomatin* came nobly into port with all sails set, after a wonderfully short run of only eight days from Sydney. Mrs Selwyn very well indeed and blooming. The people here think she is so much younger than the Bishop."

The Waimate Mission Station, which Selwyn had chosen as his first place of residence, was situated about 15 miles from the coast. It had been a Church Missionary Society settlement for the past eleven years. There were many reasons why the Bishop had decided upon this particular place. In the first instance it was a well-established mission with three solidly built houses and several cottages, schoolrooms and workshops. The CMS missionaries had spent ten years of hard labour clearing the bush and cultivating the land. At the same time they had established close links with the Maori who attended the church and the schools in considerable numbers, even though there had been some decline in recent years.

A distant view of the Waimate Mission Station about 1835. An engraving from the original by S. Williams published in the Church Missionary Register, April 1836.

Furthermore its relative isolation appealed to him. He argued that his work there would not be harmed by the low moral tone of the towns and his plans would not be hampered by previous practices. By choosing the Waimate he was able to shelve the decision as to whether his headquarters should be at Auckland or Wellington. Lastly he was not over-committing himself financially, as he had been able to rent the whole mission station for a modest

William Charles Cotton MA
1813 - 1879
Priest, Missionary and Bee Master

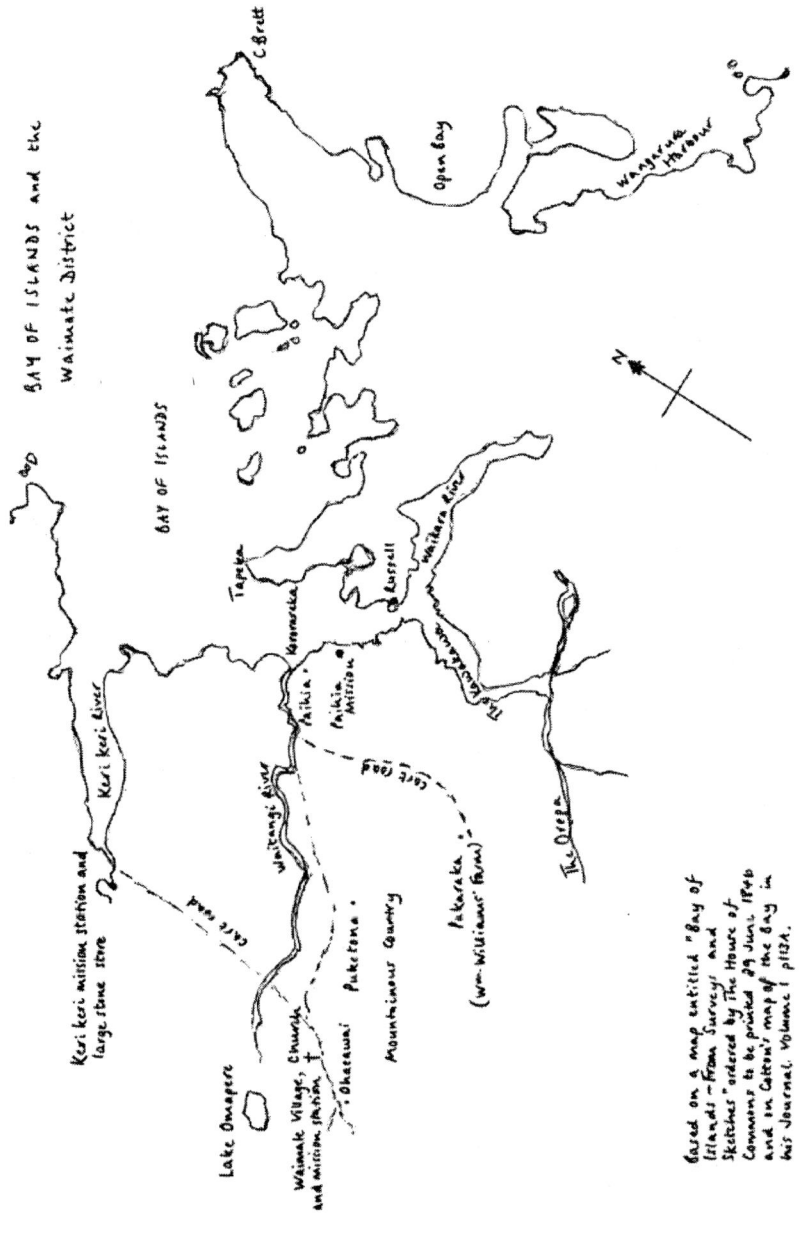

£400 per annum. There was enough accommodation for the entire party at the settlement, so their baggage was sent there immediately, but the Bishop's furniture and books were deposited at the stone storehouse at Keri keri - which afterwards became the diocesan library.

In his account of the mission station, Michael Standish describes the Bishop's first impressions as follows:
"His first sight of Waimate was at night. The large white church with its tall tower gleamed softly in the moonlight. The houses and cottages, with their lighted windows, presented the appearance of settled comfort and reminded him of England. But the next morning when he walked round and gave the place a close inspection he realized that all was not well and much work was needed to restore and develop the mission station for his needs."[1]

Of the three houses built by the missionaries, Selwyn chose for his residence the house next to the church - the one furthest to the West and formerly the home of George Clarke and his family. Clarke had left in 1840 and since then the house had remained uninhabited. By the time Selwyn arrived it had become dilapidated and badly in need of refurbishment. So he immediately gave instructions to the carpenters to carry out some basic repairs before Mrs Selwyn arrived from Paihia.

William Charles Cotton MA
1813 - 1879
Priest, Missionary and Bee Master

Sarah Harriet Selwyn

Mrs Selwyn had regarded it as only the normal duty of a loving wife to accompany her husband to New Zealand, even though her son, Willie, was only an infant. In her "Reminiscences" she wrote very little about the hardships of the five months voyage, except to say that life on board was very crowded. But, she commented, "happily it was before the extinction of poops and airy stern cabins," which suggests the accommodation had not been too uncomfortable for her.

When Bishop Selwyn decided that he and Cotton would go on ahead of the rest of the party, he had left his wife and infant son in Sydney. When, a few weeks later, Mrs Selwyn crossed to New Zealand she must have dreaded the thought of landing in a strange country and finding herself alone. One can readily appreciate her relief when, on reaching Paihia, she quickly recognized her husband in one of the boats wearing his familiar shovel hat.[2]

Selwyn had only arrived at the Bay a few days before and now there was a large gathering of natives on the beach full of curiosity to see the Bishop and to give Mrs Selwyn a lively welcome. This is how, many years later, she described the scene:
"Haere mai, Haere mai Mata Pihopa" - "Come here, come here, Mother Bishop," the whole party pressing round to shake hands which was a long process. I felt shy at airing my Maori learning before such numbers and indeed the business in hand, or rather hands, left little time for further amenities, there was such a forest of them on either side."[3]

Mrs Selwyn's joy at being reunited with her husband was short-lived because, after only two weeks, the Bishop left for a six months tour of his new diocese. He had begun the series of prodigious journeys for which he became famous. By January 1843 he had travelled 2685 miles - 1400 by ship, 397 by boat, 126 on horseback and 762 on foot.[4]

For the most part he thoroughly enjoyed his new life, often trekking across country, camping out and then sailing great distances around the coast and across to the islands.

Sarah Harriet Selwyn An engraving by F C Lewis from a painting by George Richmond. By kind permission of the Hocken Collections, Uare Taoka o Hakena, University of Otago, Dunedin, New Zealand.

After staying at Paihia for a few days, Mrs Selwyn made the journey inland to the Waimate. Before describing her arrival and Cotton's role there in the ensuing months, perhaps it would be useful to sketch in a little of the background to Maori society and of this particular mission station.

William Charles Cotton MA
1813 - 1879
Priest, Missionary and Bee Master

The Maori in the Early 1840s

When Bishop Selwyn came to New Zealand the Maoris had a relatively simple way of life but with a rich cultural heritage. However they had developed a system of agriculture and domestic manufacture that generated a considerable amount of trade between the tribes and the European settlers. As with all native societies some features of their life were regarded as admirable whilst others were condemned as cruel and barbaric. The most notorious of their former practices was cannibalism, which had become part of the ritual of celebrating victory over an enemy.

By the early 1840s thanks to the courage and unstinting hard work of the missionaries, many of the tribes had converted to Christianity and most of these cruel practices had been abandoned. But, as we have seen, just prior to Selwyn and Cotton's visit to meet, Teraia, the Maori chief, in May 1842, he had slipped back into his old barbaric ways. Fortunately he had behaved himself during their visit. Ernest Dieffenbach travelling in North Island in 1841, reported that "this frightful custom" had not entirely disappeared. Yet great progress had been made in the last two decades as Mary Martin made clear in this passage from her book **"Our Maoris"**:

"The New Zealanders were just emerging from barbarism and had, in our part of the country, only ten years before, been wild impulsive heathen. The old picturesque dress...... had given place to slop trousers and a blanket. A quainter spectacle one could hardly see than a party of men squatting in a half-circle with their blankets drawn round their bodies, and hiding every part of their faces except a bit of tattooed forehead and a pair of bright eyes. Then, whatever the habits of this people had been in their warmer ancestral home in the tropics, they eschewed much washing. Hands and blankets betokened that soap was a luxury. Their clothes had a combined scent of fish and tobacco and wood smoke. But we found them on acquaintance to be an independent, rough mannered, merry, kindly race, often obstinate and self-willed, yet very shrewd and observant, and eager to learn English ways .... It was very pleasant to hear from our open windows the chatter and laughter of the people as they ate their meal *al fresco*; and, later on in the evening, and in the still early morning, the sounds of hymn and prayer."[5]

Mohi and a Young New Zealander from Mary Martin's book "Our Maoris."
Mohi, a huge fellow, first visited Mrs Martin as a patient.
When his wife died he came to live on their ground. Mrs Martin described him as a "wild, huge and grotesque-looking but loved by all English children."
The young New Zealander was a typical chief who had attended an English school, worked for the settlers and lived on equal terms with ordinary people.
Mary Martin "Our Maoris" page 89.

Cotton gave similar descriptions of the changes taking place in the dress and customs of the Maori in his letters and journals. The picture overleaf can be found in Volume IV of the Journal, along with his observations which are summarized on the next page.

William Charles Cotton MA
1813 - 1879
Priest, Missionary and Bee Master

Changes in the dress of the Maori. Journal Volume IV page 10.
Dixson Library, State Library of New South Wales.

The gentleman on the right, says Cotton, could well be a London physician. He is wearing a blue shining gambroon coat, which is such a good fit that it must have been made for him, and a black satin stock. From his ear he has a shark's tooth hanging by a black satin shoe ribbon. "This is a favourite ornament of the Maori and, with this exception, he would not excite any notice were he to walk the streets of London. His continuations being in perfect keeping. He wears shoes and stockings also." The other man is a handsome looking fellow, fully tattooed. He is wearing a fine mat that Cotton had thrown over his shoulders, as the Bishop's chaplain thought it to be a far more becoming dress than the sheet which he had arrived in.

William Charles Cotton MA
1813 - 1879
Priest, Missionary and Bee Master

The Waimate Mission - a Brief History

Charles Darwin had visited the Waimate in 1835, and had been very impressed with it. On 21st December 1835 the *Beagle* had sailed into the Bay of Islands. After his boisterous welcome in Tahiti, Darwin found the Bay of Islands very quiet and unimpressive, and the natives dirty, disagreeable and inhospitable. The one bright spot for Darwin was his arrival at the Waimate.

In his book "Voyage of the Beagle" he described his visit as follows: "At length we reached Waimate. After having passed over so many miles of an uninhabited useless country, the sudden appearance of an English farmhouse, and its well-dressed fields, placed there as if by an enchanter's wand, was exceedingly pleasant.................At Waimate there are three large houses, where the missionary gentlemen, Messrs Williams, Davies and Clarke, reside; and near them are the huts of the native labourers. On an adjoining slope, fine crops of barley and wheat were standing in full ear; and in another part fields of potatoes and clover."[6]

Darwin continued his account of the settlement with a lengthy description of the various kinds of vegetables, fruit and flowers growing in the nearby gardens. The farmyard had stables, a threshing-barn, a blacksmith's forge, and on the ground ploughshares, not to mention a number of pigs and poultry. At a little distance stood a large water mill. He commented that all this was all the more remarkable when it was remembered that five years ago nothing but fern flourished there.

The Reverend Samuel Marsden, a long-serving member of the Church Missionary Society, had established the Waimate Mission in 1830 on his sixth visit to New Zealand. A central committee in London administered the Society and district and local committees looked after the missions overseas. In New Zealand, however, the authority of the local committees was overshadowed by the Reverend Samuel

William Charles Cotton MA
1813 - 1879
Priest, Missionary and Bee Master

Marsden, who was a powerful and much respected figure. By the mid 1820s he had set up several mission stations on the coast - in 1814 at Rangihoua, Keri keri in 1820 and at Paihia in 1823.

A sketch of the Waimate Mission House from W Yate's "Account of New Zealand" published in 1835.
The flag bears a cross and a dove carrying an olive branch, with the words "Rongo Pai," which means Gospel - a sign for all of peace and love.

Each of these stations was run on more or less the same lines. The members consisted of one or more ordained clergymen and a number of lay missionaries or catechists. The latter were tradesmen, for example, farmers, blacksmiths, carpenters or weavers, who not only carried out their missionary duties but also taught the Maori their trade. For many years the question was often debated which should come first - the teaching of the Christian faith or giving instruction in a particular craft. Reverend Marsden believed that practical training should precede religious education for "the learning of these crafts would divert the Maori from their fiercer pursuits and wean them from what appeared to him to be their unhealthy habits of living."[7]

*The CMS was an Anglican body founded in 1790 to carry the Gospel to distant lands.

William Charles Cotton MA
1813 - 1879
Priest, Missionary and Bee Master

By the late 1820s Marsden became convinced that the risk of any Maori hostility had greatly diminished so that the missionaries could move beyond the coast. For some years he had thought the Waimate might be a suitable site for another mission station. There were a large number of Maori living nearby and the great chief, Hongi Hika, had his principal cultivations there, which included the growing of maize, kumaras and potatoes. There was plenty of timber and running water in the numerous streams. In addition it was a good distance from the rowdy distractions of Kororareka, where visiting sailors might lure both missionaries and Maori into evil ways in the grog shops.

At a meeting of the full committee of missionaries, held towards the end of March 1830, it was agreed that a new station should be established at Waimate. It was hoped that such an inland mission would become an example of farming enterprise and show the natives the way forward, and at the same time be a granary for the missionaries themselves. It was certainly an ambitious project and would require great courage and determination to carry out.

After some debate it was decided that those selected to found the station should be the Reverend William Yate as the resident clergyman, with the help of the lay missionaries George Clarke, Richard Davis and James Hamlin; Hamlin was a weaver by trade, Davis a farmer and Clarke a gunsmith. Beyond the cultivated parts, the ground was covered by tall fern and scrub, and Davis was to spend many years in arduous back-breaking work superintending the development of the mission farm.

The chosen site was on a plateau above a gently sloping rise running east to Puketona and west to Lake Omapere. To the north the land sloped down to the Waitangi River and to the south towards Ohaeawai. Here and there were patches of trees, mostly puriri, but much of the ground was covered with tall fern and scrub. After carefully selecting the spot for the settlement and purchasing the land from the Maoris,

Messrs Clarke, Davis and Hamlin set about their first task, namely to build a cart road from Keri keri - one of the first roads of its kind in New Zealand. Surveys began in April 1830 and, with the help of Maori labour, it was finished in November. It ran for 15 miles over rough country and crossed the Waitangi River over a bridge with a span of 65ft. As Michael Standish says this bridge was "something of a marvel" and, perhaps one could add, a monument to the incredible skill and hard work of these early pioneers.

Next, with the help of the Maori who rapidly became skilled carpenters, they built several small cabins that by February 1831 were ready to serve as their first dwellings. Bands of Maori were employed to cut down puriri trees and to saw them into beams, to cut planks and split shingles, while the missionaries moulded and baked the bricks. After housing their families in these temporary cottages the three lay missionaries began work on their permanent homes. Three weatherboard houses were laid out on a line running east to west and facing north. The first became the home of George Clarke and his family. James Hamlin and his wife lived in the second house, which had rooms at the back where the various schools were held. The third was built for Richard Davis who superintended the farm. The houses took fourteen months to build and in June 1832 the three lay missionaries and their families moved into them.

For a time in the mid 1830s the mission farm flourished. There were 180 sheep and good yields were produced from the 40 acres of wheatfields. In 1840, a record season, over 71,000 pounds of flour was ground in the mill.

The Mission Schools

At first the Maori were hesitant to come to the church and schools but once the ice was broken they came in considerable numbers. Why? Because they loved the singing and the discussions on scripture. The lessons appealed to their love of oratory and debate, and they liked the hymns and the music. Michael Standish claimed, "the magic letters and numbers opened up great vistas of undreamed of knowledge - it was all fascinating. Unexpected and apparently almost miraculous success crowned the missionaries' efforts, at least for some time."[8]

Soon they had established a number of schools at the Waimate operating simultaneously. There was a school for men, youths and boys, one for women and girls, and another for infants. Besides these formal schools, there was training going on all the time on the farm, in the houses and in the carpenter's shop. School rooms had to be built for all these eager scholars and although completely accurate numbers are impossible to know, Standish gives these figures: in the period 1831 to 1836 between 74 and 120 men and boys, with approximately the same number of women and girls were being taught at the schools. In addition there were large numbers of others who attended the Sunday Schools or who came for religious instruction.

The Waimate was New Zealand's first full-scale European-style farm. Throughout the early 1830s the settlement flourished. Wheat was grown to supply the other mission stations with flour. The Maori attended the church and mission schools in large numbers. Many accepted Christian teaching and gained experience of English methods of farming. In its heyday it was a large and thriving village. The English crops, fruit and vegetables, pigs, poultry and the mill, greatly impressed Charles Darwin in 1835.

Unfortunately Maori interest in the mission began to decline in the late 1830s and numbers attending the church and schools dropped away. Many of the native people left, preferring to apply their newly acquired skills to their own land rather than working for a pittance on the mission farm. One of the final blows for the schools arose out of the accidental death in 1840 of a little Maori girl who attended the infants' school. Her death occurred whilst she was living in Clarke's house, and a party of Maori led by Hone Heke came to make enquiries. They were not satisfied by the explanation given, and a noisy uproar ensued and Heke left taking many of the mission Maori with him.

A Naturalist's View

Ernest Dieffenbach, a naturalist to the New Zealand Company, visited the Waimate in 1840 and made some interesting observations. In his book, "Travels in New Zealand" published in 1843, he wrote that the Waimate, with its "very European aspect, has a church and nearby are the houses of the missionaries, which are surrounded by rose trees and other plants of foreign extraction. There is a great want of flowering plants in New Zealand and imported ones improve the landscape." "In the neighbourhood," he stated, "are the poor and slovenly huts of the natives, forming rather a painful contrast."[9] However when he saw the natives in church on the Sunday, he thought most of them were cleanly dressed in the European style and the work of "Europeanising" them seemed to be gradually progressing. However he claimed that, although the Waimate was a convenient spot for a mission station on the road to Hokianga, and for the southern and the northern districts, it was not a good place for agriculture. He described the soil as "very light dusty volcanic earth." "This is the reason," he stated "that the natives have no plantations here, but prefer the ravines intersecting the plain, or go nearer to the groves, or to the base of the hills which bound the table-land where the soil is more substantial."[10]

He went on to say that the Maori who lived in the area belonged to the Nga-pui, which was formerly one of the largest tribes in New Zealand. But in recent years they had greatly decreased in number, despite the ascendancy, which the conquests of E'Ongi gave them over many other tribes. They had become much dispersed in their small villages. Remains of their ancient *pas*[11] were visible on the hills in the neighbourhood of the Waimate.

It would seem from Dieffenbach's observations that it is not at all surprising that the mission's heyday was fairly brief, with the poor quality of the soil and the decrease in the number of Maori families living in the district. As a consequence the mission farm had gradually proved less and less economic, especially as many of the Maori who remained had chosen to grow their own crops. All this meant that it was far cheaper for the missionaries to import flour from New South

Wales. Another reason for Maori disenchantment was their growing suspicions about the European acquisition of their lands. For these reasons, the numbers attending the church and schools declined in the late 1830s, and although Richard Davis struggled on farming the land, output dropped as he found it increasingly hard to recruit Maori labour. This is why Bishop Selwyn found the mission in such a rundown state when he arrived in June 1842.

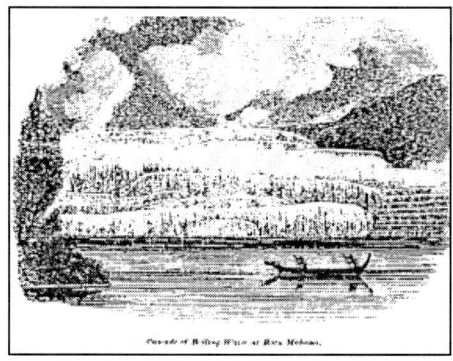

"Cascade of Boiling Water at Rotu Mahana" from the title page of Ernest Dieffenbach's book "Travels in New Zealand" 1843.

NOTES AND REFERENCES - CHAPTER THREE

[1] M W Standish "The Waimate Mission Station" page 28.

[2] A type of clerical hat favoured by Anglican clergy at the time.

[3] Sarah Selwyn "Reminiscences" page 17.

[4] Una Platts - "This Lively Capital" page 103.

[5] Mary Martin "Our Maoris" page 8-10.

[6] Charles Darwin "The Voyage of the Beagle" page 409

[7] M W Standish "The Waimate Mission Station" page 11.

[8] Ibid page 19.

[9] Ernest Dieffenbach MD "Travels in New Zealand." 1843.

[10] Ibid page 248.

[11] Fortified villages.

CHAPTER FOUR

LIFE AT THE WAIMATE

Cotton's Duties at St John's College

In the light of the decline in Maori interest, it is not surprising that when Mrs Selwyn arrived at the Waimate, like her husband before her, she found the place in "a sad state of decadence." The garden had been trodden over by cattle and had degenerated into a wilderness. The house into which they moved had been badly neglected and had become very dilapidated. Extensive repairs had to be undertaken which continued during the next twelve months. The roof shingles needed to be totally renewed and the chimney completely rebuilt which meant the kitchen could not be used for months. After long delays the new oven was ready in October but the roof was not finished until March 1843. In addition to these repairs, partitions were built on the upper floor to make more rooms. It is hard to imagine how Mrs Selwyn and Reverend Cotton managed to cope with all the mess and inconvenience that this work must have caused. But Sarah Selwyn was a stoical character. She never complained about or regretted leaving England - on the contrary she remained cheerful and good tempered throughout this difficult time.

William Charles Cotton MA
1813 - 1879
Priest, Missionary and Bee Master

A sketch of the Bishop's house at the Waimate after the repairs and alterations had been completed in March 1843.
Journal Volume IV p.106. Dixson Library, State Library of New South Wales.

In the Bishop's absence Mrs Selwyn and Cotton were to be in charge - a responsibility that must have weighed heavily on her. Though she speaks of him as a likable character, she found he had an erratic disposition and sometimes she doubted his ability to measure up to the demands likely to be made of him.

In her "Reminiscences" she describes her arrival at the Waimate and gives her thoughts on Cotton's role there:
"A house being vacant and the Society agreeable for George to begin here, he took possession of the Mansion, our first New Zealand home, so for this place on the 6th July I started with Willie and Nurse[1] in a cart, escorted by the aforesaid Mrs Taylor after taking leave on July 4th of my husband for six months......

William Charles Cotton MA
1813 - 1879
Priest, Missionary and Bee Master

The rest of the younger staff were to be left at Waimate under the care(?) of Mr Cotton. There was no doubt of his ability and willingness to take every possible care of us. His great inequality of spirits at intervals and other things made him often a great anxiety to me, for fear of what he might do, but I might have spared my fidgets, for no son could have been more considerate or kind or attentive than he was to me in that long six months."[2]

When the Bishop sailed for Auckland on 5th July 1842, with William Evans as his travelling companion, he was starting out on his first visitation which was to last six months. Two colleagues accompanied him - Robert Cole and Charles Reay who were bound for the missions at Wellington and on the south east coast respectively. Later Selwyn planned to visit Nelson and the mission stations at Rotorua, Torepo and Mata Mata.

Two days after her husband's departure, Mrs Selwyn took possession of the empty house. Situated next to the Church, this was the house that had been hurriedly made ready as the Bishop's residence. In those first weeks Sarah Selwyn and WCC were grateful for the hospitality afforded by Mrs Taylor, the wife of the Reverend Richard Taylor. The Taylors lived in the adjoining house and helped the newcomers with furniture, bedding, meals and in many other ways.

In a later passage in her memoirs, Mrs Selwyn tells us more about her first impressions of the Waimate:
"On reaching the Waimate we found some cleared fields with cattle in them and grass growing around the weather-boarded houses...... The house we were to inhabit seemed odd to me at first. I felt as if I was living in a box - floor, walls and ceiling all of wood - not panelled or adorned. We had the piano up from Keri Keri - the first effect of which was, when I played, to make a benevolent old visitor in a blanket think I had got a man inside clamouring to get out."[3]

William Charles Cotton MA
1813 - 1879
Priest, Missionary and Bee Master

The original plan had been that Cotton, as the Bishop's domestic chaplain, would accompany Selwyn on his various journeys but unforeseen circumstances had meant he had to take on different responsibilities. His colleague, Reverend Whytehead, had become seriously ill in Sydney and was unable for the time being to travel to the Bay of Islands. He was to have been the headmaster of the school at the Waimate. Cotton now had to take on this position in addition to his other duties of lecturing, preaching and looking after the Sunday schools.

In a letter to his sister, Sarah, dated 19th July 1842 he wrote: "Well, then, I am now head of the family at Waimate, Principal of Bishop's College, Divinity lecturer, Classical lecturer, officiating minister at St John's Church, Waimate, and half a hundred things besides, but all in the way of business." And later he added "here I am, striving to do my bit, feeling that I have got "promotion" and most happy that Mrs Bishop is Mrs Selwyn for as the Bishop said at parting "he had full confidence that we should get on well together."

Church Services

Within ten days the new arrivals, in co-operation with the CMS clergy and catechists, were ready to hold regular Sunday services in the church. Most of the congregation consisted of Maori and soon Cotton and his colleagues had organized a Sunday School for the settlers' children. In addition, from 18th July, they began to hold daily services, some of which were conducted in the native language. As one might expect only a small number of people usually came in the weekdays but the Maori often attended in great strength on Sunday mornings. At one of the first services, there were 285 communicants, who were mostly natives. It is difficult to imagine how the clergy coped with so many people even though the church was larger than one might have expected. Early in August 1842 Cotton recorded: "The congregations, however, on Sunday, are between three and four hundred and make the responses as one man."[4]

William Charles Cotton MA
1813 - 1879
Priest, Missionary and Bee Master

A few weeks later he described how a problem sometimes occurred with the taking of the wine. The communion table stood on a small platform, with only a narrow step up to it. As there was no communion rail, the natives mostly leant on both their hands or squatted down. Consequently the administration of the cup was not very easy or very seemly. With all these communicants, the service, which began at 9-30am, often did not finish until after 1-00pm.

On most occasions during his stay in New Zealand Cotton showed a great affection for the Maori people. After some of his first church services at the Waimate, speaking of the large Maori congregation, he described them as "a very fine sight." "They make their responses capitally" he declared "But oh their singing! It's regular Aclandian phrase yelling. They are a finer set of people, than I anticipated, and they improve everyday on acquaintance."[5] His study of the Maori language on board the *Tomatin* soon paid off and in church he was not only reading prayers but preaching fairly fluently in the native language.

Besides taking church services, WCC was busy teaching a small number of students for holy orders. One of his other tasks every day was to deliver a Greek Testament lecture. On Monday 21st August he took the Church service at 8 o'clock, with a congregation of seventeen, and then gave his lecture as usual. However he had to finish at midday because the new kitchen chimney was not finished and the dining room was needed to prepare the dinner. It is interesting to note that throughout his stay in New Zealand, Cotton wore a cassock in church and a cassock and silk gown when teaching in the College. Writing home some months later he pleaded with his sisters to send him some new clothes as his old ones were becoming threadbare.

During their first few months at the settlement, Cotton lived in the Bishop's house and used the study as his room. When Whytehead arrived late in 1842, the study and bedroom became his quarters. At this stage WCC moved next door into rooms in Hamlin's old house, at the rear of which the lessons and lectures took place. This house had been christened "Eton College" but soon in 1843 it was renamed "St John's College." About this time Selwyn decided that, in keeping with the best traditions of the Oxford and Cambridge colleges, everyone should dine in hall. By everyone he meant himself and his family, his chaplain, candidates for holy orders, the masters and pupils in the various schools and the college servants.

At the same time Mrs Selwyn, in a more modest way, began to exert her authority and insist on certain rules in the "Bishop's Palace." She believed that it was very easy for her colleagues to fall into lazy habits in these far-flung colonial places and so she began to demand high standards of dress and demeanour. This is how, some years later, she described her feelings on the subject:
"So we assembled in evening attire at our tea without milk and our bread without butter and made ourselves agreeable according to our lights and behaved "pretty" as the (children's) nurses used to say."[6]

On Wednesday 24th August everyone was given a holiday to celebrate St Bartholomew's Day - except for WCC who was expected to give his Greek Testament lecture as usual. In the afternoon of Saturday 27th August, he went over to Mr William Williams' farm at Pa Karaka. There the eldest Mr Williams walked with him to a spot near the extinct volcanic cone of Pourua where they found a strong emission of gas and numerous small swampy pools.

After his morning teaching the young men, he regularly took Mrs Selwyn and young Willie for a walk. Mrs Selwyn, in her "Reminiscences," says that they always included a stretch on the road to Kororareka to see if there might be a messenger bringing them news from the Bishop or from England. Letters in the first twelve months were rare. Once they found a box had arrived. They waited with baited breath for it to be opened but, when it was, they found only two shovel hats inside.

William Charles Cotton MA
1813 - 1879
Priest, Missionary and Bee Master

Meanwhile the Bishop had reached Nelson where he was holding regular services and doing everything possible to help the church to prosper there. On 23rd August he wrote to Cotton: "Your father's tent is now actually a Cathedral with a daily Maori service, morning and evening." Then he added the interesting remark: "I feel more in my office here than I have felt anywhere, with the entire command of my own services. I wish you were with me."

The First Honeybees

It is a well-established fact that there were no hive-bees in New Zealand prior to 1839. There were two native species but neither was any use as honeybees. The person who undoubtedly deserves the title of New Zealand's first beekeeper was the aptly named Mary Anna Bumby. In 1838 she agreed to accompany her brother, John Hewgill, when he decided to take up the position of superintendent of Wesleyan missions in the colony. They arrived at Mangungu, Hokianga Harbour, on 13th March 1839 in the sailing ship, *James*, with two hives of bees that she had obtained in Sydney. It is thought that they were the black or "German" type, or perhaps more accurately called the North European bee. These were the first honeybees to be brought to New Zealand. (see Appendix III)

In 1840 Lady Hobson made another shipment of bees, also from New South Wales. As far as we know Cotton was not aware of the introduction of these bees into New Zealand. During his stay in Sydney in April 1842 he had made good use of his time and befriended a number of beekeepers. No doubt he had related the story of how he lost his bees on board the *Tomatin* and his friends had promised to send over some hives once he had settled down at the Bay of Islands.

A few months after the Bishop's party arrived at the Waimate, Cotton helped with the work of re-establishing the gardens and planted a small part of them with thyme, in readiness for the arrival of his first stock of bees. Some time later he built a small bee-house to shelter his future hives.

William Charles Cotton MA
1813 - 1879
Priest, Missionary and Bee Master

Miss Mary Bumby who brought the first honeybees to New Zealand in 1839

Willie Selwyn

During the six months that the Bishop was away, Cotton developed a great fondness for the Selwyn's infant son, Willie. On a number of occasions he described him as a fine boy or a most amusing fellow. Once, probably with his head of flaxen curls in mind, he called him the "charmingest" of boys. He loved to quote Willie's sayings, for example, when describing their usual daily diet as mainly potatoes and water, he wrote "or as Willie calls it poa and wawa."

Writing to Edward Coleridge in August 1842 he described Willie as "a most magnificent little fellow." He explained that the boy had learned to walk during the voyage and was now getting on well with his talking. However, Cotton added that, on his arrival, he had been "sadly rude" to the little missionary children, "pushing them all over like a pack of cards." This behaviour no doubt arose from his experience on board ship where he probably imagined "he was the only boy in the world."

During the Bishop's absence Cotton was given the office of "the putter up of posts," that is, it became his job, when Willie was crying, to raise his forefinger as a signal for him to stop. As the months went by, WCC repeatedly showed his delight at the boy's progress. In November he wrote that Willie was making a "great show of his talking" and that he had a good ear for music. He loved to sing songs like "Isle of Beauty," "Froggy" and "Buy a Broom." Without a doubt Cotton took a great delight in his singing and enjoyed his lively character.

Towards the end of December 1842, Mrs Selwyn was trying hard to stop Willie from sucking his finger. Cotton had provided some finger stalls (fingers of a glove with a tie attached) which were in constant use. At the same time Mrs Selwyn had also tried putting mustard and then aloes on the offending finger. The former he just licked off and said how nice it was. The latter he disliked and called it "nasty stuff." The finger stalls would not stay on, so as a last resort, his mother wound "plaister" round and round his finger. The first evening she did this he tried sucking his other fingers, but they would not do, so he spent a very restless night. As with most children, Willie was slowly persuaded to desist and the habit became a thing of the past.

Another time Cotton was delighted with the boy's wonderful memory. One day when Willie was playing with an old jigsaw puzzle, he was impressed by the way he could recite the names of all the animals from the elephant down to the mouse. However, Cotton observed, he did have some difficulty in distinguishing the tiger from the panther.

One day in early August WCC walked after dinner with William Nihill[7] to a wood where the sawyers were at work cutting some kauri planking to repair the Bishop's house. He wrote later "the forest consisted generally of tawai; here and there might be seen a majestic Rimu pine, or rata, bearing crimson flowers. There were many aborescent ferns, and in the deepest shade grew the Nikau palm."

William Charles Cotton MA
1813 - 1879
Priest, Missionary and Bee Master

The Arrival of Reverend Whytehead

On Sunday 16th October 1842, as Mr Taylor was away at Keri keri taking Holy Communion, Cotton had to conduct all four services at the Waimate - though Mr Davis did help with the Maori preaching. Later that day, in a letter from Henry Williams, he learnt that Reverend Whytehead had arrived in the Bay of Islands. After a stormy passage lasting some ten days he had come over from Sydney in the *Bristolian* and landed at Paihia.

Mrs Selwyn was overjoyed when she heard of Mr Whytehead's imminent arrival. She wrote later that the news "lifted such a sense of responsibility (from me) and brought the thoughts of pleasant companionship and cultivation and refinement and goodness to benefit our little circle."

Another part of their missionary duties was to conduct services in the nearby native settlements. In mid October Cotton went with Mr Davis to the Whare Karakia. On arrival they entered a very neat "tapa" or reed building which had a thick bed of long leaves covering the floor. Inside there was an attentive congregation of about forty natives. He read the prayers and Mr Davis preached. Usually there were about one hundred in the congregation but, on this occasion, many of the Maori were away at Hokianga planting potatoes. Mr Davis had been visiting this settlement for the last twenty years.

By the end of October Whytehead was still on the coast at Paihia. On Monday 31st October, though it was a cold day, they decided to go for him. Cotton wrote "William Hau came for orders...... He was so tidily dressed that we had him in for breakfast. He sat at table and behaved quite like a gentleman." He had brought his men and soon they set off for Paihia. On arrival there it was agreed that the Maori should carry Mr Whytehead in a litter. It consisted of two springy poles about 15 feet long, in the middle of which was a seat with low sides made of koradi. The two bearers popped their heads between the two poles that rested upon their shoulders. Altogether there were six bearers who, in turns, undertook the task of carrying the sick man. Whytehead lay on the litter with his carpet bag at his back and coats laid over him. At first he was nervous at this unaccustomed form of travel but after a while he relaxed and enjoyed the experience. The journey took about three hours. About half a mile from the Waimate a number of folk met them on horseback. Cotton observed that they "were like a party chairing the successful candidate after a general election," with Major Richmond heading the procession. Everybody was very happy to have Mr Whytehead with them again, and the native bearers were regaled with two large dishes of Maori soup. They all sat down on the grass encircling the dishes and "spooned away to their hearts content."

Everyone at the Waimate must have quickly realized that Whytehead had only a short time to live. Cotton wrote: ".......for he is a mere shadow. But still it is a great blessing to have him amongst us once more though it be but for a time." During the next few months Whytehead tutored the CMS veteran, Richard Davis, for ordination and worked with the latter's son, James, on the translation into Maori of Thomas Ken's "Evening Hymn."

Towards the end of the year Mr Whytehead's condition began to deteriorate even further. When Selwyn heard the sad news he decided to return to the Bay of Islands as quickly as possible. During his first six months in New Zealand the Bishop had visited nearly every one of the CMS mission stations in North Island. To everybody's delight, especially that of Mrs Selwyn and Willie, he reached the Waimate on 9th January 1843. Cotton had spent the day riding down to the store at Keri keri to collect some books for Reverend Whytehead. In one of his letters he describes how he heard the news of the Bishop's arrival: "I got back to the Waimate by 7-30. And as I was walking my horse leisurely up the field I saw Wm Watts tearing down to meet me, so I cantered on to meet him. Two words regularly knocked me off my horse, and set me scampering over the field faster than any part of my ride. They were, as you may imagine, "Bishop's come."[7]

In the weeks following his return the Bishop several times expressed his appreciation of Cotton's hard work during his absence. Not only for the diligent way he had carried out his teaching and ministerial duties but also for being such a good companion to Mrs Selwyn.

The Church Font

One of the special events that took place early in 1843 was the unpacking and setting up of the Church font - a gift from Cotton's sisters in England. In a letter to Sarah and Phoebe, WCC described how the font had been brought to the Church at the Waimate. He expressed great anxiety lest it had suffered any damage during its long journey. He feared that the cases had undergone a great deal of extra banging about when the *Tomatin* was under repair at Mosman's Bay in Sydney. Then they had been transshipped to the missionary schooner, *Columbine*, and brought up the Keri keri river but had remained in the store there for six months during the Bishop's absence. Finally, he wrote, "to test the packer's skill to the uttermost, it (the font) was jolted along in a dray for ten miles over a road, such as no other country but New Zealand would call a good cart road."

At last the long-awaited day came for the font to be unpacked. On Friday 20th January, after Morning Prayers, everyone gathered round to watch the opening of the wooden cases. When the cover was lifted off an avalanche of sawdust poured out but the onlookers were relieved to see there were no fragments of stone with it. When they cleaned away the remaining sawdust, the font was found to be in perfect condition. As there was no west door, it was placed in the centre of the church at the intersection of the two aisles. Soon the carpenters had measured out the exact spot for it, bored a hole through the floor and fixed a lead pipe to carry the water away. Cotton later wrote of his intense relief that all his fears of damage had proved to be unfounded and the Bishop expressed his great delight at this handsome new addition to the Church - the first stone font in New Zealand.

At the same time a beautiful altar cover, made by the Misses Watson, was put in place. A poor box - a copy of an old one at Oxford - was also fixed close to the door. Unfortunately Mr Whytehead was not well enough to witness the unpacking of the cases, but he came into the church the next day. He was overjoyed to see the beautiful font and the fine new altar cloth.

A service taking place at St John's Church, the Waimate. Note the pulpit given by Bishop Selwyn, and the stone font donated by the Misses Cotton. Journal Volume III page 71. Dixson Library, State Library of New South Wales.

In addition to the font another gift arrived at the church early in February 1843. On the fifth Sunday after Epiphany a new communion plate was used for the first time. The clergy and parishioners of Windsor had given this beautiful silver plate. On that day there were twenty-eight communicants and the alms amounted to £4 - 4s. Also for the first time chants were included in the service. They had eight men's voices and could choose the best of the boys' voices. Cotton reckoned their choir would soon be "as good as any second rate cathedral." Since the Bishop's return the number of Maori attending the afternoon service had greatly increased.

William Charles Cotton MA
1813 - 1879
Priest, Missionary and Bee Master

The Bishop's Lodge

On Monday 30th January Archdeacon Henry Williams of the Church Missionary Society paid a visit to the Waimate and a great many Maori came to see him. In the evening the Bishop arranged a korero in the dining room. Cotton wrote: "It was a grand thing to see all their mahogany faces lit up with pleasure when he (the Archdeacon) went in to see them."

At the rear entrance to the Bishop's house or, as Cotton sometimes called it, "the Episcopal Palace," stood a small lodge with a gate. On the sign post by the gate the Bishop had ordered a notice to be posted. Wata, one of the Bishop's Maoris, was delighted to be made "the registrar of the Episcopal laws," and undertook the posting of notices and, no doubt, the guarding of this rear entrance. In return he was allowed to live in the lodge.

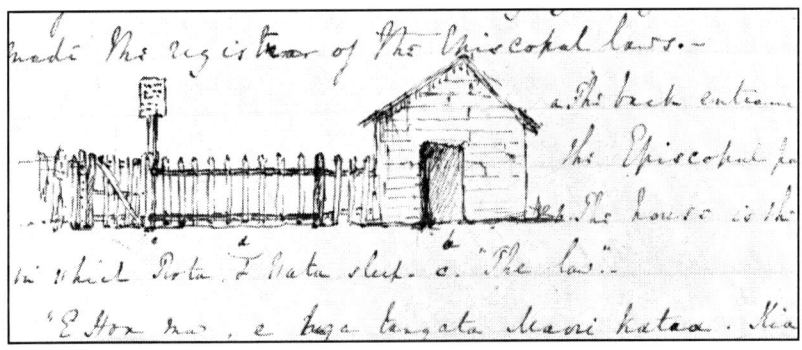

A sketch of the lodge. Journal Volume III page 173. Dixson Library, State Library of New South Wales.

Above the sketch Cotton copied out the notice. As it was written in Maori, he gave the following translation:
"Oh my friends, oh all ye Maori men. Listen to me. Cease smoking (literally eating) and bringing Pipes into my place. When you come here, leave your pipes outside, and don't come here smoking your Pipes, lest you set fire to my house. Law of the Bishop of New Zealand."

On Monday 6th February 168 Maori came to the church and the school. During the morning the Bishop catechized them on the subject of prayer. Cotton stated that Selwyn had already succeeded in drilling the whole school into very much better order. Clearly his presence made a considerable difference to the attendance at church and the response of the children in school - further evidence of Selwyn's charismatic leadership. Finally that afternoon a large "market" assembled in the grounds of the Bishop's house. The following note in Cotton's Journal suggests that young children could be a problem at these gatherings: "The Bishop's second law against the women bringing pekanis has as yet been entirely inoperative."

The Bishop's House and Grounds

At this time work was still continuing on the repair of the Bishop's house and it would appear that Cotton was lending a hand. On 14th February he noted that they "got all the ties and rafters fitted and pinned - a good mornings work." Meanwhile the Bishop was busy marking out the "pleasance" in front of the house. Cotton acted as "surveyor's assistant" and they laid out an ellipse-shaped lawn. Rota, whom the Bishop called "Capability Brown," did all the spade work and was delighted with the design. In the rather grand way of the learned Bishop and his erudite chaplain they decided to create what Cotton called "a living orrery," that is they used a layout based on a clockwork model of the planetary system. In the next few weeks they planted a variety of trees and shrubs - tree ferns, karakas, nikaus and other native plants mixed in with privet and acacia - as part of this ambitious scheme.

In mid February WCC had bought two native mats to send home. One, that had a fringe, was meant to be worn like a shawl. The other was more finely made and intended for use as a table cover. So pleased was he with these purchases that he requested the captain of the missionary schooner to buy him two more mats at the East Cape, as the Maori no longer made them in the northern part of the Island. To produce them required a great deal of labour and the natives could buy blankets more cheaply. Cotton thought they were a poor substitute for the hand-made mats. He declared, with some feeling, "they have been entirely superseded by the filthy European blanket. The natives have suffered both in appearance and health by the change." (see Appendix V for more information about Maori dress).

But, he thought, in recent times the demand for English clothes had become so great that he hoped the "blanket may return to its nightly use." In fact when the Maori attended the Waimate church more than half of them wore European clothes - shirts, trousers and maybe coats, but at times their choice could be rather bizarre. "An old pair of dress trousers will be topped by a red jersey shirt but," he wrote, "I need not go through all the possible combinations of the odd clothes which ever were found in Monmouth Street."[9]

The missionaries soon realized that the Maori would benefit from some instruction in making their own European-style clothes. In this way they would not be so dependent on buying imported garments, many of which were of poor quality and quickly fell to pieces. It is not surprising, therefore, that Selwyn wanted to provide sewing classes to enable the natives to make their own clothes.

Later in the month the Bishop held his first confirmation service. 328 Maori were confirmed which shows the extent of the teaching that Selwyn and his colleagues were undertaking and the progress they were making.

The Library at Keri keri

When the Bishop's party first arrived at the Waimate, Selwyn used the stone storehouse as a depository for some of his baggage and equipment. After a while he decided to convert one or two rooms to house his collection of books. Mrs Selwyn called it the "Cathedral Library." Undoubtedly Cotton always enjoyed his visits there. He described it as "the most comfortable room in all New Zealand" and added "The constant music of the Keri keri cascade, not ten yards from the building has a soothing effect............ I know no better place for a good Day Dream than the Keri Keri Library."[10]

William Charles Cotton MA
1813 - 1879
Priest, Missionary and Bee Master

A drawing of the mission house and stone store at Keri keri, showing the nearby waterfall on the river. Journal Volume VIII page 182.
Dixson Library, State Library of New South Wales.

A reading group at St John's Collegiate School - 7th July 1844.
Journal Volume VII page 177.
Dixson Library, State Library of New South Wales.

William Charles Cotton MA
1813 - 1879
Priest, Missionary and Bee Master

St John's College

On his homecoming Selwyn stated that he found the St John's College, Waimate, "already established" with the following members: tutors - Reverend Whytehead and Reverend Cotton and six students. However the date often given for the official opening of the College is 15th March when, according to Allan Davidson,[11] the students for holy orders were: Seymour Spencer, Christopher Davies, Henry Butt and William Davis, with Frederic Fisher, William Nihill and Thomas Williams as junior members. Offices were assigned to the students, with Spencer and Fisher acting as senior and junior bursars, Butt as curator of the hospital, Nihill as sacrist and curator of the press and Williams master of the walks.

The Bishop noted in April 1843: "St John's College is now open with seven students - all duly arranged in caps and gowns - a goodly sight they are in Church and a goodly hearing, too, for they chant the Psalms most reverentially."[12] In July he recorded that the students were "going through a course of Divinity Lectures with me and of Greek with Mr Cotton, besides lectures in the native language, medicine and Latin."[13] He regretted that the regularity of these lectures had been interrupted by the illnesses of Mr Whytehead and Mr Dudley.

The founding of such a college had been one of Selwyn's earliest ambitions. The mission schools had existed for some time but he had wanted to establish a college that, he said, would be a "place of religious and useful education for all classes of the community, and especially for candidates for holy orders."[14] He hoped that these candidates, when ordained, would serve as future missionaries or work with settlers in their communities.

From the outset St John's had three main departments: the College itself, for candidates for holy orders; the Collegiate School, formerly the CMS English Boys' School, established for the sons of missionaries and other pakehas, which met in the middle house (sometimes called Eton College); lastly, in the third dwelling, which Cotton described as a sort of Magdalen Hall, the married candidates lived. By May 1843 there were five married men in hall. All new Anglican clergy coming to New Zealand were expected to reside at St John's to learn Maori and to stay for at least two terms.

From the beginning Selwyn had laid down the general principles of the College, which included the rule that everyone had to spend a proportion of their time in useful work. This was deemed necessary both to generate a good community spirit and to try to make St John's self-supporting. At this stage the only regular income of the College was £300-00 a year from the Society for the Propagation of the Gospel, plus the Bishop's and Cotton's incomes which they had both pledged to the College. Under the "industrial system" at St John's every student was required to practice one active and one sedentary trade. For example the older students were employed in gardening - tilling the soil and growing vegetables. At other times they were busy helping Thomas Williams who had the task of laying out the College grounds. Or they were assisting the Bishop with his schemes for planting lots of native trees. Besides the gardening and farming work, as mentioned earlier, a small printing press had been established and, in 1844, a spinning and weaving school was started.[15]

In addition to requiring all his colleagues and older students to take part in this "industrial system," the Bishop expected everyone to lead an austere and simple life. This applied particularly to their meals that were served and eaten communally in a large room at the rear of Eton College. The Bishop and Mrs Selwyn, Whytehead, Cotton and other clergy sat at the high table. The students for holy orders and their wives dined at a second table, the schoolboys at a third and the servants at a fourth. The College Kitchen was based on the plan of a kitchen at Cambridge, that is, it supplied regular "commons" to every member and "sizings," that is, extras to those who ordered and paid for them. "Commons" which included meat, bread, potatoes, tea and sugar, cost one shilling per day. Mrs Watts was the College Cook. With the help of a few assistants, she baked and cooked for the whole College.

William Charles Cotton MA
1813 - 1879
Priest, Missionary and Bee Master

The Death of Reverend Whytehead

For some months Cotton had slept on a sofa in Whytehead's day room so that he could render any assistance that might be required. During this time he watched his friend slowly wasting away. In the last few weeks of Reverend Whytehead's life, Cotton looked after him nearly every night, with help from the Bishop and, especially from Mrs Selwyn, in the daytime. For a fortnight Cotton undressed him and put him to bed, and then attended to his needs during the night. On the morning of 19th March 1843 he found such a change in his friend's appearance that he called the Bishop immediately. Selwyn asked for a prayer book and, shortly after he had read a few prayers, Whytehead passed away.

During this sad day there were the usual four services in the church. Cotton stated that on each occasion the Bishop arranged everything beautifully to suit the circumstances. In his sermon to the Maoris, Selwyn related how he had just come from the bedside of his dear Brother, who only last week had sent them the "Himene Hou," his translation of the Evening Hymn and who was now listening to this new song in Paradise. On 21st March Reverend Whytehead was buried in ground very close to the church. Cotton explained "when the projected chancel is built he will lie under it." With the death of Whytehead, the Bishop had lost probably his most able lieutenant - a fact that was, unfortunately, to be reflected in the shortcomings of St John's College in the next few years.

Maori Children

In a letter written to his sisters at this time Cotton expressed his delight at the singing of the Maori children. He said that their singing in school was excellent and had improved enormously since the Bishop's party had arrived at the Waimate. They picked up a tune very quickly and their singing in Church was equally impressive. William Bambridge, about whom Cotton was quite scornful, gave the music lessons. He wrote that Mr Bambridge "has all the conceit that characterizes such dedicated people, specially folk whose half education was in the musical line."

Mrs Bambridge also came in for some criticism. He claimed she had never done anything for the general good since leaving England, and that she devoted the whole of her time to domestic duties. She spent many hours "cooking nice little delicacies for the small gourmand, her husband, who like many total abstinence men, makes up for the restraint put upon one appetite by the indulgence of the other." Finally he declared that they should never be listed in the Society for the Propagation of the Gospel's publications as schoolmaster and schoolmistress.

The Collegiate School

After the death of Whytehead, Cotton was asked to take charge of the Collegiate School. As stated earlier, until this time he had lived in the Bishop's house but now his new responsibilities required him to take up residence in Eton College. He regretted not living with the Bishop and Mrs Selwyn anymore, but he could still visit them in the evenings, after 8 o'clock, when the boys had gone to bed. It was then, he stated, that he enjoyed a very nice "coze" - a hot drink, a warm fire and good company.

George Butt, a clergyman who had arrived several months before in the *Medusa*, served as under master in the school. Cotton did not think very highly of Mr Butt and his wife. He stated that he was only resident there because of the extreme silliness of his wife, which had prevented the Bishop from sending him to look after one of the mission stations. Cotton called him "a sad creature," and added "I pity him, but I cannot like him." Eventually Thomas Hutton, who was recruited by Selwyn's brother, William, took over as assistant master. There were also schools for Maori teachers, Maori boys and girls, and a few months later, classes for infants were started.

Many years later Mary Martin wrote this description of these Maori schools:

"We often visited the native girls' school, which was under the charge of a clergyman's wife. She had taught them to spin flax, and they were very merry over their work, and sang many of our school songs amid the whir of wheels. The infant school was delightful - plump, jolly Maori children, who clapped their hands and sang the multiplication-table with great glee. New Zealand children are pleasant to teach, they are so wide awake and full of fun."[16]

William Bambridge taught the Maori boys. On Monday 13th March he noted "I received a new scholar this morning and taught him the English alphabet. I was surprised......one half hours application and he mastered the whole in large and small characters." But he went on to write "The difficulty is in keeping them in School. They are so accustomed to be free and apparently disapprove of the least confinement." Furthermore the boys objected to a diet of potatoes served to them for breakfast and supper and of rice and sugar for dinner. They were quick to point out that at their kaingas they were accustomed to a variety of food. Despite these problems, Bambridge was impressed by the enthusiasm and ability of his pupils, writing "I cannot see any reason why in 6 months time they should not be able to read tolerably well."[17]

On Monday 24th April Bambridge was busy going around collecting the names of the students in the various classes. One of the classes that he visited was a group of about twenty young and middle-aged women who were sitting on the vestry floor and being taught by Mr Cotton. Bambridge wrote: "Rev Cotton's was a very amusing class." Apparently when the first woman gave her name, the others burst into laughter. Soon everyone was laughing and it was difficult for the teacher to restore order.

Towards the end of 1843 the students of the College consisted of four married men, three single men, eleven native boarding school boys (dressed in the school uniform of blue linsey), the native Girls' School pupils and seven boys of the Collegiate School. On 18th September a Maori infants school was started with Elisabeth Colenso and Marianne Davies in charge. By April 1844 the number of students attending the various schools had reached 80.

William Charles Cotton MA
1813 - 1879
Priest, Missionary and Bee Master

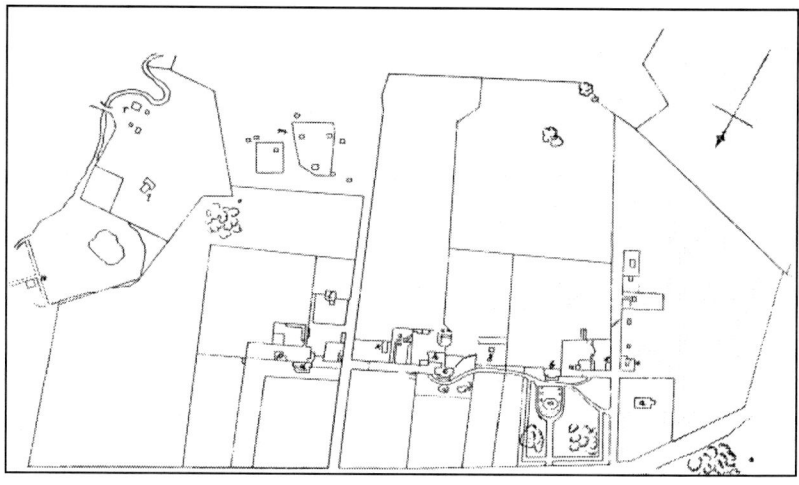

A plan of the Waimate settlement in 1843.
The building shown as "St John's College and Palace"
was formerly George Clarke's house.[18]
Dixson Library, State Library of New South Wales.

a. The Church
b. St John's College and Palace
c. Eton College
d. Magdalen Hall
e. Mr Spencer's
f. Church Street with Tenements
q. Mr Bedggood's
g. The New House
h. The College Hall
i. Mr Bambridge's
j. Mr Colenso's
k. Play House - to be an Infants' School

l. Barn
m. Maori houses
n. Mill & Pond
o. Tapu bushes
p. Maori School
r. Blacksmith's Shop
s. Hospital
t. Printing Office & Carpenter's Shop
u. Robert Hussey's Shop
v. Wood House

William Charles Cotton MA
1813 - 1879
Priest, Missionary and Bee Master

"Servant of All Work"

In April 1843 WCC expressed his lack of enthusiasm for his new position, even though he was glad to show willing and undertake whatever tasks were given to him. He wrote: "school keeping with the missionary children for pupils is not exactly the work I should have chosen, had I had the choice, and chosen to exercise it. This perhaps the Bishop knows, but we are much straightened for hands. He has no one to put into the school, so until a regular schoolmaster comes out from England (and I do not care how soon he comes) the servant of all work cannot do better than keep his place warm for him, or rather I should say keep his boys warm."[19]

Clearly Cotton didn't believe he was suited to this work. After all he had agreed to accompany Bishop Selwyn as his chaplain, not as a schoolmaster. However it was to his credit that he was prepared to step into the breach and teach the missionary children. Or as he recorded "he was glad to be able to show that his willingness to do anything he was asked to do, was more than just talk."

In the light of these admissions it is not altogether surprising to find that after a time some criticism arose with regard to Cotton's teaching. Although he was a genial and affable character, he seems sometimes to have lacked the ability to teach his pupils in an orderly manner. Joseph Matthews of Kaitaia stated that:
"the Bishop's College at St John's ..... went on so badly and so wildly under poor Mr Cotton that parents were afraid to send their sons to that college and the Visitor Judge Martin interfered and told Bishop Selwyn that this work must cease as it had become a public scandal."[20]

Allan Davidson takes the same view of Cotton's inability at times to cope adequately as a schoolmaster:
"While Williams and others appreciated his many qualities such as his friendliness and practical ability and his special care for the sick, they

were concerned about Cotton's emotional instability, and his competence as teacher in charge of the English Boys' School. His assistants Hutton and Dale also came in for criticism. Hutton was described as a "sour man" and Dale was criticized for his heavy handed corporal punishment, of which Selwyn did not approve."[21]

At the same time that this criticism was being levelled against him, certain people were praising him. For instance Canon James West Stack recalled that when he was a new boy at the mission school, Cotton was "the most kindly and genial of men, brimful of fun and good humour, who soon set me at ease."[22] In addition Selwyn commended him for his willingness to undertake these duties. In a letter dated 4th July 1843 he declared:
"Mr Cotton is most invaluable to me, being willing to do anything and everything, and doing all with steadiness. In fact without him I should be utterly unable to carry on my present operations."

Relations with his father

By April 1843 Cotton seems to have been on better terms with his father. Writing to his mother he stated that the latest letter from his father "had done his heart good," though he still felt his father showed a lot of "doubt and mistrust." WCC admitted that there had been good cause for this in the past, but expected that by now the Bishop's letters about his work at the mission would have dispelled any remnants of doubt in his father's mind. He quoted the Bishop as saying only that day: "That it was only from the good providence of God that I was with him." Undoubtedly Cotton felt much happier with his role at the Waimate than he had done in his last few years in England. In fact he probably found it hard to imagine how he was going to tear himself away from these tasks when the time came for him to leave New Zealand.

A few days later, in a letter to his father, he explained how, from the start of the voyage, he had placed his money in the Bishop's hands, drawing on him now and again when he needed to. He was pleased to say that this arrangement had worked well and was glad that his father had not mentioned the subject in his last letter but had waited to hear from the Bishop. Evidently these financial arrangements, and the circumstances of his life at the mission, had held in check any urge to over-spend that he might still have felt.

At the end of May 1843, he was still desperately waiting to hear that his father was reconciled to the step that he had taken. Cotton hoped that the letters which the Bishop and Mrs Selwyn had recently sent would persuade his father of his reformed character and valuable work at the Waimate.

The Printing Press

About this time, in addition to his many other duties, he began to look after the College printing press. It had been a struggle to get the press into working order because, for one thing, the type had become completely muddled during the voyage from England and it needed a lot of laborious work to sort it out. By April 1843 Cotton had instructed two workmen in how to operate the press and they were busy producing various printed papers for the Church and College. For instance, he mentioned that they had found it useful to give the Maori a printed summary of the Bishop's sermon to take home. By the middle of April they had printed the first volume of the College calendar. One big advantage of having their own press was that it made the Bishop independent of the Mission Press at Paihia, which pleased him greatly.

Writing in May 1843 Cotton stated, "he wished his sister could see our office of the Printing Press in active operation............ Nihill is an excellent compositor, and Wm Watts, pressman. The Bishop is very anxious to get out a good almanac for the Maori and there are several books he would like to publish for them." Finally, he declared that the flourishing state of the printing office had proved wrong those friends who called him a "Tom Noddy" for bringing his "little press" in the first place.

A Special Occasion

In the summer of 1843 arrangements were made for the Bishop to ordain Richard Davis on Trinity Sunday. As noted earlier, he had laboured long and hard as a CMS Catechist at the Waimate. After his many years of diligent work with the Maori both in the fields and in their religious training, Davis was "anxious to receive this regular commission and to act upon it in the remaining years of his life." On the appointed day, such was their respect for Richard Davis, the Maori came to the church in great numbers. The Bishop conducted the ordination service in Maori and everyone was delighted to see the old man raised to the priesthood.

William Colenso

In June 1843 William Colenso, a CMS Catechist, took up residence at St John's College and became the Bishop's "Professor of Maori."[23] In the mid 1830s he had been sent out from England to set up a much-needed printing press at the Paihia mission station. He lost no time and, within days of his arrival, he had the press ready for operation, though printing had to be delayed because of a serious lack of certain items of equipment and a shortage of paper. But ingenious ways were found to overcome these problems and soon he was printing Biblical texts for the mission and notices for James Busby, the British Resident. Colenso's greatest achievement during his stay at Paihia was probably the printing of a Maori version of the New Testament - the Reverend William Williams providing the translation. Bagnall and Petersen, in their biography of Colenso,[24] state "it is not easy in these days of modern printing to appreciate fully the great task involved in compositing the whole of the New Testament (some 356 pages) in Maori and printing 5000 copies, largely without help and on a small hand press that would feed only two octavo sheets at a time. The undertaking occupied Williams and Colenso from the 14th March 1836 to 30th December 1837." It was a truly remarkable achievement and one that would make a significant difference to the mission and to the Maori people.

William Charles Cotton MA
1813 - 1879
Priest, Missionary and Bee Master

By the early 1840s William Colenso began to find his duties at the printing office extremely irksome. For many years he had taken a great interest in natural history and during his few "holidays" from Paihia he had set out on expeditions to study the flora and fauna of the East Cape. He had used these visits to meet and converse with the native people, seeking always to extend his knowledge of their way of life, language and culture. At the same time he had become convinced that it was time for him to find himself a wife. After considering the daughters of four of the missionaries and finding none suitable, a friend recommended Elizabeth, the daughter of Mr Fairburn who ran the mission station at Otahuhu. Once again he tried the approach that he had used unsuccessfully with Henry Williams' daughter. He wrote to Mr Fairburn enclosing an open letter to Elizabeth. This time his entreaty was successful and it was agreed that they should be betrothed. Selwyn, who had heard of Colenso from Bishop Broughton, was told of his plans to marry Elizabeth Fairburn. The Bishop, who knew of her ability and experience as a teacher of Maori girls, now urged an early marriage so that the couple could come to the Waimate - Elizabeth to take charge of the Maori Girls' Boarding School and William to study for holy orders. Though Colenso did not always see eye to eye with the Bishop (as his religious predilections were Low Church), he fell in with the Bishop's suggestions. On 27th April 1843 he married Elizabeth and on 13th June the newly wedded couple arrived at the Waimate.

Both William and his wife were to find life at the Waimate very exacting. Elizabeth in trying to make the native girls, with their carefree customs of the pa, conform to pakeha standards and to the sometimes unsuitable rules of the boarding school. Whilst William had to cope with several arduous tasks: his studies for ordination, translation work for the newly established printing press and divinity classes. Mrs Colenso wrote the following description of their busy daily life:
"First then at half past 6 a bell rings to summon folks out of their beds. At seven is the breakfast bell when a servant from each house goes to

the 'College Kitchen' to get meat and bread for their master's breakfast, 1lb of bread and half a pound of meat being their allowance for each person. At 8 every morning except Sunday the church bell rings and all have to attend to hear the prayers and lessons of the day read - the students have to read the lessons alternately - it is generally over by nine and when the Bp. is at home the gentlemen have to attend at Divinity, Greek and Maori lectures which are seldom over before one o'clock - when his Ldp. is out they have only to attend Greek lectures by Revd.. W C Cotton at 12 o'clock - the intermediate time being taken up in preparing for the same - at 2 the dinner bell rings when all have to dine at the 'College Hall'...... all dine at the same time and we seldom exceed twenty minutes at dinner - it is regular kaihoro work I can assure you - at 5 every evening the Church bell again rings and at 8 is the curfew or concluding bell for the night....."[25]

Much of the time Colenso did not enjoy his stay at the Waimate, mainly because he disagreed with the High Church sentiments of the Bishop and his party. In his autobiography he described Cotton as Selwyn's "eccentric High Church Chaplain" and was disdainful of the Bishop's entourage, especially "several newly arrived ladies with their own peculiar and unsuitable notions."[26] As a consequence of his strongly held views and resulting clashes with Selwyn, it took him a lot longer to gain his ordination than he had expected.

Friendship with Mrs Selwyn

In July 1842, when the Bishop had left on the first tour of his new diocese, he had asked his chaplain to take care of his wife and young son. From all accounts Cotton had carried out this duty most assiduously. We have seen how he regularly accompanied Mrs Selwyn and Willie on walks in the mornings and spent a good deal of time with her in the evenings in conversation, reading and writing letters. In one of her letters Mrs Selwyn made these comments on his role at the Waimate: "Of this place Mr Whytehead had been the main prop; but it was too fixed to be altered and Mr Cotton took his place, with that abandonment of self, which is the great charm of his character, for it was indeed an exceeding disappointment to him to forego the long journey with the Bishop." She went on to say that WCC believed that Selwyn had left him in a "responsible position" and the "promotion" had consoled him. She concluded "I have a very good character of him ready for his Master when he comes home."[27]

Early in May 1843 Cotton visited Mrs Selwyn at Mr Taylor's house at Pa Heke about two and a half miles from the Waimate. He explained that, at times, she suffered from severe headaches. Unfortunately they had one or two quarrelsome servants in the household who created a great deal of tension. Hence her desire to get away for a couple of weeks.

After spending so much time in her company, Cotton came to regard her like an older sister. Referring to his family at home in Leytonstone, he wrote: "But I only hope you are all as happy as I am. I did not think I would ever have loved any one, at least with a few exceptions, so very dearly as I love Mrs Selwyn. It must certainly be an advantage to a man to have an elder sister. My younger sisters do very well, but few elder sisters, I fancy, can come up to Mrs Selwyn."[28]

In another reference to her, he wrote "no epithets can be good enough, or express all I feel towards her, so I omit them altogether."[29] He often described Mrs Selwyn as cheerful and in good spirits, but, as mentioned above, she sometimes suffered from "sad headaches," aggravated by disputes with the servants. One person who troubled her greatly was her footman, Arnold. Cotton described him as impertinent and lazy, and "a regular discontented grumbler, unwilling to carry out any duty which he did not think strictly within the province of a footman." As a matter of fact what worried Mrs Selwyn most about this troublesome servant was that it would fall to her husband to deal with him and that would cause the Bishop great anxiety. Eventually Selwyn did tackle the problem and Arnold was sent home to England.

William Charles Cotton MA
1813 - 1879
Priest, Missionary and Bee Master

As the years went by Cotton became more and more fond of Mrs Selwyn. In a letter to her dated 4th March 1844 he addressed her as "my dear mother" and finished with "Ever your most loving son." In a note to his sisters he explained that there had been no opportunity to send this letter to Mrs Selwyn so he was sending it home to give them more news. Finally he made the following telling remark: "You see Mrs Selwyn has formally adopted me as her son, in consequence of many requests from me." It is possible that his close relationship with Mrs Selwyn, and to some extent with the Bishop, fulfilled a need for love and care, which he had not found with his own mother and father. At the same time his deep regard for the Selwyns, along with other good friends, must have made his departure from New Zealand in 1847 all the more harrowing, even though he hoped to return.

The Expedition to Otana

On 20th July 1843 Cotton set out on his first tent expedition. Selwyn had decided that after his extensive visitation, it was time that some of his colleagues took their turn to visit the nearer mission stations. Cotton had been asked to make the twenty-mile journey to Otana to meet the local people and to take Holy Communion there. William Bolland, a student of the College, who had been stationed at Taranaki for some time, accompanied him. Their other companions were three Maori who were carrying the tent, blankets and food. They were Renata Kawepo, Isaiah Miataki and Te Tora Temora - all of them good friends of WCC. One can readily imagine the five of them trekking through the New Zealand bush engaged in lengthy conversations in Maori and, as Cotton wrote, "learning more of the native language in one journey than in a month's quiet residence at Waimate."

The worst of such journeys on foot in winter was the mud. Sometimes, especially in the woods, it came over their knees. The Maori took off their "combinations" and waded across the marshy ground in their shirts. The two Englishmen, determined to maintain their dignity, rolled up their trousers above the knee. They spent their first night at

William Charles Cotton MA
1813 - 1879
Priest, Missionary and Bee Master

Kaikope about twelve miles from the Waimate. The Maori pitched the tent for them and they slept on fern beds that Cotton thought would be springier than heather. Some of the fern was quite wet but he used a large sheet of Macintosh to cover it and, in spite of heavy rain, they had a comfortable night.

This is how Cotton described the scene that greeted him the next morning: "I turned out of the tent just before the sun rose, and a most wonderful view met my eye. A curtain of mist was hanging on the (hills) about half way down. This curtain gradually drew up, leaving little bits of clouds like detached picquets in the different hollows. The sun came out. Our tent steamed rapidly and our thinks (sic) were hung out to dry."[30] The following day they trekked through the bush and reached Otana before nightfall. They found the Maori of the pa very hospitable. On their arrival they were given a meal of freshly boiled potatoes and tea made in a saucepan. During their stay the natives fed everyone so plentifully that the visitors had no need to eat any of their own supplies. On Sunday 23rd July the Maori assembled for their evening karakia or prayer. They met in the largest ware belonging to Wiremu Kapa, the principal man of the settlement. Cotton described the gathering as follows: "There were about 50 people present and it was a most striking scene as all their dusky faces stood out from the darkness, lit up by the one candle, part of our travelling equipment, from which I was reading (the scripture and prayers)."

Early on Monday morning he went to visit two sick persons. The first was an old woman who was lying in the last stage of illness in a very small hut. A large fire filled the hut with smoke, which made his eyes water excessively as he read prayers from the visitation for the sick. Cotton called her "a great sinner who showed no signs of true repentance" and, consequently, was not allowed to receive Holy Communion. The second person whom he visited was an old man. He found him in a comfortable state and permitted him to be a communicant.

On his return to the tent they ate a bowl of rice with sugar for breakfast and then started out for the Ware Karakia for their morning service. On the way they had to cross a stream where the water was knee deep. To save his "blacks," (presumably his black trousers) Cotton reluctantly agreed to be pekaned over by his friend, Renata Kawepo. "We were soon assembled in the chapel," he wrote, "which was a very neat reeded building holding about 70 people. It was nicely strewn with wheat straw. There was a Table and four or five benches for the principal people. The commonalty sat on their heels in a position which is quite natural to them, but which would give dear Mama a back ache to look at. It was a most orderly congregation and I had 42 communicants, including our two selves and our three Maoris."[31]

The next morning they started out on their return journey. Cotton was up before sunrise. They had eaten their breakfast and had the tent struck and packed by 8-15am. On their way they found the rivers and streams much swollen by the rains and were glad when the Maori found an old canoe to transport them across the largest stretch of water. They reached Kaikope at 1 o'clock and the Waimate three and a half hours later, again at times walking through deep mud.

The Bishop's Second Tour

Cotton had complained for some time that he had not had a break from his duties at the Waimate, except for his few days in Otana. Early in October 1843 the Bishop gave him the opportunity to have a longer change of scene. At the start of the summer vacation he set out with Selwyn on his second episcopal visitation, which turned out to be a lengthy expedition to the mission stations and native settlements in the southern part of North Island. One of their main objectives was to learn about the numbers and condition of the Maori who lived on the shores of Lake Taupo, especially as Selwyn intended to leave Mr Spencer in charge of a mission there.

William Charles Cotton MA
1813 - 1879
Priest, Missionary and Bee Master

William Nihill, a nineteen-year-old clerical student, who had come out with the Bishop from England, accompanied them. The rest of the party consisted of Maoris, whose main tasks were to carry the baggage, paddle the canoes, pitch the tents and prepare the meals. Their knowledge of the bush and the geography of the country, and their familiarity with the language and the people, were to prove invaluable.

William Nihill.

Ink and blue wash by William Bambridge.

Ms-0131-043, Alexander Turnbull Library, Wellington, New Zealand.

The party started from the Waimate on 4th October 1843 bound for Taurarua Bay, Auckland, where the Bishop left Mrs Selwyn and Willie in the care of Mrs Martin. From Auckland they canoed for some distance up the Thames river, but then leaving their eleven Maori boatmen, they set out to walk the 330 miles to New Plymouth on the west coast. After spending some time in the Taranaki district, they set out again and visited Rotorua and Lake Taupo. Half way down the eastern shore of Lake Taupo, the Bishop established a camp at which they spent several days. Here on Sunday 5th November a special event took place. William Martin, the Chief Justice, who had set out on his own expedition some months before, arrived with his party after travelling up from the south. Such was the care both men had taken over these matters, that they met on the exact date that they had arranged months before.

Mary Martin described in detail how such an expedition travelled: "A merry party of natives carried a supply of flour, sugar, rice and biscuits and some beans on their backs, besides blankets and a light tent. For the rest the whole party depended on the hospitality of the Maori who gave freely from their stores of potato and fish to the Manuhiri - the Stranger. Sometimes a pig could be bought and the men, however heavily laden before, cheerfully carried a quarter of pork on their backs."[32]
Usually the midday meal consisted of pancakes made lighter by the addition of potatoes and sweetened with brown sugar.

At Whanganui Selwyn decided to split the party into two sections, so that between them they could cover more of North Island. The Bishop took charge of the first group and Cotton led the second one. In Cotton's party the leader of the Maori was Renata Kawepo.

Renata Kawepo. A drawing by T B Hutton.
Journal Volume V page 197 A. Dixson Library, State Library of New South Wales.

William Charles Cotton MA
1813 - 1879
Priest, Missionary and Bee Master

An interesting aspect of this expedition is that, in addition to Cotton's account, Renata wrote his own description of the journey, which must be one of the oldest surviving pieces of extended prose by a Maori. Almost certainly he wrote this account at Cotton's request and the text can be found in Volume VI of the Journal. It has been transcribed in copperplate on the top half of each left hand page and extends to sixty-five pages. His full narrative has recently been translated, edited and annotated, by Helen Hogan and published, along with a detailed commentary, in her book "Renata's Journey."

Cotton's party spent some weeks in Otaki and Wellington and, after visiting Nelson and New Plymouth, returned by the west coast to Kawhia and then through Auckland back to the Waimate. Such expeditions were extremely arduous and this one was no exception. Most of the time the men were either travelling on foot or in canoes or small sailing boats. They had steep cliffs and mountains to climb or sometimes marshy country through which to wade. Their diet was fairly limited and often food became extremely scarce. Here are a few incidents on their journey, recorded by Renata, and quoted from Helen Hogan's book:

"So then we set up the tents and when that was done we cooked the meal; there was one pig and we divided it up with the loin and the legs for the Pakeha, the belly for us."[33]

Tuesday 13th February 1844 "In the morning we set off and came to a steep climb, a cliff. The way up was a rope let down from the cliff. We climbed and got to the top, and then we walked until we got to a river."

Thursday 15th February "Cotton and Haira fell. People called down to them to keep holding on. Then I climbed up calling up to them to keep holding on. When I was close I took his arm, held on to him, and carried him on my back. Cotton protested vehemently.....Cotton's trousers were all torn with the rocks."[34]

William Charles Cotton MA
1813 - 1879
Priest, Missionary and Bee Master

The title page from Volume VI of the Journal, showing WCC and one of the Maori (probably Renata Kawepo) in their expedition clothes.
Dixson Library, State Library of New South Wales.

William Charles Cotton MA
1813 - 1879
Priest, Missionary and Bee Master

Cotton's Leadership

In her book Helen Hogan makes some interesting comments on Cotton's qualities as a leader. Whereas everyone accepted Bishop Selwyn's authority, when the party split up and WCC took over the direction of his group, Renata frequently questioned his decisions. For instance, on their way to Mangapouri, they came near to Kakepuku. Here he decided to make a detour to visit the Wesleyan missionary, Thomas Buddle. Renata objected to this plan because he felt it would cause unnecessary delay. It was not usual for Cotton to pay social visits to Wesleyans but he was received cordially. They were served with coffee, bread and butter and eggs - a much-appreciated treat after a week in the bush.

Sometimes he accepted Renata's advice about when to stop for the night but at other times he ignored his suggestions. Another disagreement arose over Cotton's wish to visit Taranaki to see his friend, William Bolland. This proposal angered Renata, because the detour would add many miles to their journey and he was suffering with a painful leg. These incidents are interesting for the light they shed on WCC's leadership. Although on such expeditions some arguments were bound to arise, the number of times this occurred shows perhaps a lack of forcefulness in Cotton's character.

During their visit to Taranaki, an incident occurred which is worthy of note. One evening three Maori arrived at the parsonage, dripping wet from the rain. They had walked ten miles from their pa to visit Mr Bolland. The first thing their hosts did was supply them with some dry clothes. Mr Bolland provided one of them with an old silk cloak and Cotton gave the other two a cloth cloak and a "P.Jacket" (a working coat). After a meal the Maori squatted down by the door and explained their problem. In their village there were two churches - one Anglican and one Wesleyan. A good deal of trouble had arisen from the ringing of the bells for services. If one church waited for the other to finish ringing before they started, then they would be disturbing the service in the first church. After giving the matter careful thought, Cotton and Bolland advised that the best solution would be for both churches to ring their bells at the same time. Cotton then wrote out this advice in Maori so that they would have a letter signed by Mr Bolland to take home to show their people. He began the letter as follows:

"E Hoa ma e te hunga mote Haki kei Hausanga.
Gena za ko kawton katoa. Tenei anotaken."

"O friends and the people of the Church of Hausanga
How do you do. This is my book to you."

The Bishop's Return

After being away for nearly three months, Selwyn returned to the Waimate on 22nd March 1844. His wife and son had remained with Mrs Martin at Taurarua, near Auckland. He arrived there early in March and then, after a short stay, the family sailed in the Government Brig, *Victoria*, for the Bay of Islands.

Cotton had returned to the Waimate a few weeks before. In a letter to Mrs Selwyn, he explained how Nurse, Ann Stapley, had looked after the "Bishop's Palace" so well in their absence. "Tho the roof was off during torrents of rain, not a single thing has been injured - all owing to Nurse's great exertions." "But" he wrote turning to another matter, "none of the native trees, planted in the garden, have survived." Finally he stated that Nurse would be arranging a grand procession of the school children in their new clothes to greet the Bishop on his arrival. Evidently Ann Stapley was a capable woman, who played a significant part in events at the Waimate.

Meanwhile Cotton was busy making festive arrangements for their homecoming. After completing these preparations, he went with some of his Maori helpers to meet the Selwyns. They erected a tent as a kind of halfway house where the travellers could rest and refresh themselves. The natives helped in various ways, including making a beautiful elastic seat of Manuka (Tea tree) and then, after a while, the Maori left for Keri keri.[35] Whilst waiting for the Bishop to arrive, Cotton occupied himself in a number of ways.

William Charles Cotton MA
1813 - 1879
Priest, Missionary and Bee Master

He wrote later:
"I set a large kohua (iron pot) of rice on the fire for the natives, set out the lunch for my expected guests, wrote a pencil letter to my sisters, ... read fifty pages of Mama's kind present........which I like hugely ....corrected a sonnet or two and took a good nap."[36]

About 3 o'clock the party arrived with Willie being carried in one litter and Mrs Selwyn in another. Eagerly they came into the tent and partook of the refreshments. After about half an hour they set out again to complete the remaining five miles to the Waimate.

Mrs Selwyn travelling in one litter and her son, Willie, in another. A pen and ink sketch by T B Hutton. Cotton appended a note: "The poles are drawn wrong. They should be at the upper end of the box." Journal Volume VII page 24. Dixson Library, State Library of New South Wales.

Cotton gave the following description of the grand reception given to the Bishop when he reached the Waimate:
"At the entrance to the settlement the schools were drawn up at either side of the road, the infant schools on the right with Mr Dudley in full canonicals, ... Mr Colenso and Mr C Davies, on the other side was the Boys Schools, Native and English, with Wm. Davis and Mr Hutton. Two of the eldest girls came forward, and presented nosegays to Mrs Selwyn. They then fell in two and two, singing ABCD etc., to the tune of God Save the Queen, then followed Mrs Selwyn [who] was dismounted from her litter and put in a carriage, drawn by the four biggest boys. The rest fell in behind, so we proceeded up to the Palace.

William Charles Cotton MA
1813 - 1879
Priest, Missionary and Bee Master

The school girls scattered rose leaves on the path, there was a triumphal arch at the entrance to the Bishop's grounds so that all we wanted was one of the artists of the Illustrated News........Willie came and gave a slice of cake to each child, not unwillingly, thinking I suppose that he should get a slice at last."[37] Finally the Church bells rang for the evening service at which the Bishop gave thanks for his safe return and for his preservation during his travels.

Governor Fitzroy

Early in 1844 Captain Fitzroy, who had formerly been in command of "The Beagle," was appointed to be the new Governor of New Zealand. Almost at once the Captain and Mrs Fitzroy began to interest themselves in the education of the Maori people. One step they took was to encourage the translation of books into Maori. According to Lady Martin two of the first books to be printed at the Government press and circulated among the people were a "Life of Peter the Great" and stories from British and Saxon history. It is hard to believe that the Maori found these particular books at all enlightening!

People assembled in front of the Bishop's house for Governor Fitzroy's visit to the Waimate. Note St John's Church in the centre and the Great Tent on the right. William Bambridge. Journal Vol IX page vii.
Dixson Library, State Library of New South Wales.

In the ensuing months much more serious efforts were made to improve the welfare of the Maori. Between 30th August and 3rd September 1844 the Governor visited Bishop Selwyn at the Waimate. During his stay he held a number of meetings with the native chiefs. However in the following year serious grievances arose among the Maori at the Bay of Islands and, unfortunately, a series of disturbances took place. As a result of widespread criticism at the way he handled these troubles, some months later Fitzroy was relieved of his post.

Controversial Remarks

On very few occasions did Cotton write anything that can be said to have been critical of the Maoris. However some comments he made in a letter written on 18th August 1842 caused his correspondent, much to Cotton's intense annoyance, to send a copy to the *London Times* and to the *Auckland Chronicle*. As a result, some time later, he had the following notice printed - a copy of which is pasted in opposite the title page of Volume VII of the Journal, which he began on 2nd March 1844:

"The Reverend W C Cotton has been informed that an extract from one of his private letters has appeared in a London newspaper and in the New Zealand Journal. This breach of the laws of friendly letter writing is highly disagreeable to him and disreputable to them; and he will consider any repetition of it as concerns either his letters or his journals, tantamount to a declaration by the party so transgressing that he deserves no longer to be numbered among his correspondents."

The statements in the letter to which, presumably, his correspondent took exception were the references to the Maori. Writing about the situation of the Waimate, Cotton explained that the site had been chosen "because those at home thought that they might succeed in teaching the natives farming. But there has been little done in this respect, the people being too desultory in their habits."
However this criticism was tempered by the following positive comments:
"They are a fine race, always cheerful and ready to talk with you; and have a wonderful facility in learning to read. They teach each other so that every thing

one man learns is quickly spread all over the country. The avidity with which they ask for paha-paha or books is very remarkable, they not only ask for them as curiosities but also read them and learn them by heart." He went on to describe the church and the congregation as follows: "The church is large and built of wood. There were between 200 and 300 present yesterday. The dress of some of the ladies is rather curious. Fancy a fat old woman with a coal scuttle bonnet on her head, her face inside very much tattooed, with a bright shawl, a very fanciful printed gown, white cotton stockings, and showy sandals. This was a great chieftainess."

Then he wrote of their responses as quite astonishing. "The way in which the Maowries (sic) make the responses is singular. They all keep exactly together, so that their voices resemble a heavy surf heard at a distance. They will, I dare say, chant well some day when they are taught, but at present their singing is the most extraordinary and outrageous thing you can possibly imagine. They scream out at the very top of their voices and in some of their tunes when they go down from one note to a lower one make a most extraordinary slur, just like the sound produced from the violin on running the hand up."

Finally, with some humour, Cotton added this reference to the virtually obsolete practice of cannibalism:
"I must say the blackies are very civil. I am in no great danger of being eaten, for they are all christians (sic) here and know the Prayer book well, though I have to inform you that an old Pagan chief called Terains, whom I saw on the river, made a meal of some of his enemies the other day."[38]
Despite his good humoured, but nevertheless highly critical, comments in this letter, Cotton generally showed remarkable tolerance and understanding of what must have struck him as a very strange way of life. Furthermore, considering his comparatively sheltered background of Eton, Oxford and the Church, it is notable that he was so tolerant of many of the Maori customs and appreciative of their talents and skills.

In April 1843 he described how the Bishop had recently organized a census of the whole district. They found that there were about 2000 Maori living in the area in small, scattered settlements. He explained that, in the past, it was only wars that had forced people to live in larger settlements. Now "the Pas which used to crown every hilltop" were deserted as everyone could live in security in the valleys. With evident pride in the achievement of the churches and their missionaries, Cotton declared:"It is a wonderful thing that we should be dwelling here in the midst of a people who fifteen years ago were Cannibals. May we have the grace to build up those in the Faith for whose conversion the hand of God has been so wonderfully stretched out."[39]

The Maori often showed a deep interest in what they were being taught. For example, one day one of the Maori asked Cotton how long mankind had inhabited the Earth. Fortunately a friend came to his assistance with the answer and he wrote 5846 years on a piece of paper. His questioner then insisted on multiplying this figure by 12 to bring it to months and was not satisfied until he had worked it out in minutes.

A Long Illness

In March 1844 Alfred and Charlotte Brown, CMS missionaries at Tauranga, sent their son to the Collegiate School at the Waimate. In April 1844 Marsh Brown, whilst playing with other children, received a blow that possibly caused osteomyelitis. Such was the care he received from the College staff that Allan Davidson concludes that his treatment overcame some of the suspicion that arose between the missionaries and Selwyn's party. Jane Williams[40] stated that "Mr Cotton too greatly improves upon acquaintance and has many very good points in his character, tho' he is not what we would like to see as a clergyman and as chief master of the collegiate school. His kindness and attention to poor Marsh Brown during his long and trying illness seem to have had no bounds."[41]

In February 1845 Marsh Brown was taken back in stages to Tauranga, where, sadly he died seven months later. Shortly afterwards his parents decided to set up a scholarship at St John's in his memory and to show their appreciation of the devoted care he had been given at the College.

William Charles Cotton MA
1813 - 1879
Priest, Missionary and Bee Master

A Fateful Morning

Some months before he left England, Cotton had met Mary Eliza Hawkins. Miss Hawkins was the daughter of the Keeper of Coins and Antiquities at the British Museum in London. After a number of meetings, Cotton had fallen in love with her. When he left England in December 1841 he hoped that, after his "four years probation" in New Zealand, he would return to these shores and they would be married.

One morning early in May 1844, whilst he was busily engaged in trying to hive a swarm of bees, Cotton received two letters that brought some disturbing news. As he read the more recent of the two letters, he found that one or two sentences in the second sheet brought tears to his eyes. It was the news that he had most feared - Eliza Hawkins had placed her affections elsewhere. Later that day he wrote:
"I went on with what I was about, tho' I suppose with so strangely attended countenance, that good little D Davies, in whose garden the bees were placed, could not be persuaded that I was not suddenly taken ill."

In the afternoon he described how his students at the College, seeing his distracted appearance, probably thought he had some bad news concerning their friends that he was about to communicate to them. Later in the same letter he showed how deeply these sad tidings had affected him:
"In the afternoon Mrs Dudley kindly played to me some tune on Mrs Selwyn's piano, of which she has had the care, and big silent tears rolled down my face, and I felt relieved. As an emblem of my blighted hopes - the swarm of bees with which I had been occupied that day would not stay, but flew off and took up their dwelling in the bush."

He went on to make the following comments which show some of the problems that he faced in his relationship with Eliza and how he tried to tackle them:

William Charles Cotton MA
1813 - 1879
Priest, Missionary and Bee Master

"I am quite in the dark as to many points on which I want to be informed. What has now called forth this decided expression of 'the truth.' The arrival of Mrs Selwyn's letter to Sarah, asking for me that I might be allowed to write to MEH and giving I believe such a character of me, as would she hoped make them believe, that my days of madness were all gone by, and that a judge or archbishop could not be a more grave and reverend suitor that I should have made. Or did this kind intercessory letter go to the bottom of the sea, or at all events arrive after one that I had enclosed about the same date and I intended to be held in reserve till after dear Mrs S's had worked its end, for if it were delivered before it must have seemed like a presumptuous forcing of the blockade. All things seem to have made against me - especially the loss of the bishop's kind letter written to Papa in January 1843.

And though it must be a serious blow to have my best, and almost only earthly hope dashed away from me, do not fear that I shall sink under it. I have enough ink to keep me incessantly occupied for eight months to come, and tho' my feelings are not a wit less strong than they were some years ago, I believe that I have greater power of controlling them. I am anxiously awaiting further intelligence - at present it seems involved in great obscurity - let it be granted that MEH never loved me, or at least not so entirely and ardently as I do her, that none of the family never felt more for me than a common acquaintance, that dear Mrs Turner, no bad judge of me and propensities, did not let words drop during that memorable visit to Rooksnest in the autumn of 1841 somewhat to this effect that if I went well thro' my four years of probation, she thought that MEH would be just the person to make me a good wife, and that I need therefore not despair.

Even if no one of these things were so, it seems very strange that I should be forbidden to attempt winning her love, unless indeed she has given it somewhere else, which I could not then ascertain

to be the fact in 1841 and wait anxiously to know whether it is now. My true love is still with her tho' it may be that this severe blow is sent to me as a providential warning that God has some work for me to do, which requires that I should not be entangled with the things of this world. I shall wait the result in patience.........Well then, if it be for the last time, my sincerest love to MEH."[42]
Although Cotton had received this unpalatable news about Eliza, he did not give up hope that he still might be given the opportunity to correspond with her and in that way in time he might win back her affection.

One of the few drawings of Cotton in the Journal appears with the entry for 20th May 1844. It is a sketch by Thomas Hutton of him looking tired and dejected, which is hardly surprising since that day he had completed a 37 miles walk. He wrote: "It is not often that I have either the time or the inclination to indulge in this way, but on such an even it was unavoidable and quite excusable."

WCC resting after an extremely long walk.
Thomas Biddulph Hutton. Pencil. Journal Volume VII page 130.
Dixson Library, State Library of New South Wales.

William Charles Cotton MA
1813 - 1879
Priest, Missionary and Bee Master

A Drawn Game

Later in the winter of 1844 Thomas Chapman, a missionary from Tauranga, visited the Waimate. One evening Mr Chapman had a bad headache. Nevertheless he agreed to have a game of chess with WCC. Cotton later noted: "Mr Chapman had a sad headache this even. His first remedy was one and a half quarts of salt and water taken internally - his second a game of Chess with me - in one sense, and very nearly in another, - was a drawn game."

Mr Cotton and Mr Chapman playing chess. A pencil drawing by T B Hutton. Journal Volume VII page IA. Dixson Library, State Library of New South Wales.

A Special Day

Helen Hogan states that in Volumes V and VI of the Journal, which she studied closely, Cotton wrote lovingly from time to time of his mother but did not mention his father. However he did write regular letters to his father, and frequently mentioned him with affection in letters to other members of the family. Thursday, 12th September 1844 was his father's birthday. To celebrate the occasion Cotton decided to take all the boys on a picnic. There were sixteen in the party including one of the Maori who carried a kit of potatoes for them. They walked for eight miles down the cart track towards Keri keri until they were in sight of the waterfall. At this point they took their bearings with a compass, then struck out over hill and down dale through the high fern, and fording one considerable river, until they reached their destination.

William Charles Cotton MA
1813 - 1879
Priest, Missionary and Bee Master

At a suitable spot near a waterfall, they lit a fire and their native companion constructed a "hangi," an oven made of earth, in which they cooked the potatoes. Whilst waiting for their dinner, the boys wandered about in the wood and collected ferns and a flower from a crimson shrub. Cotton took a seedpod from the flower to send to his father in the hope that when it grew it would be a reminder to him of his birthday. After dinner they drank a toast of wine with water to his father's good health, and then they gave a lusty three cheers, which echoed round in the cavern behind the waterfall.

The site of their picnic, Cotton wrote, was one of the most beautiful spots in New Zealand. In mid afternoon they set out on the long walk back. They arrived home at about 6 o'clock, rather tired but pleased that they had completed an enjoyable walk and had celebrated William Cotton's birthday in fine style.

William Charles Cotton MA
1813 - 1879
Priest, Missionary and Bee Master

NOTES AND REFERENCES - CHAPTER FOUR

[1] The child's nurse, Ann Stapley, who had accompanied Mrs Selwyn on the *Tomatin*.

[2] Sarah Selwyn "Reminiscences" page 18.

[3] Ibid page 35.

[4] Letter dated 2nd August 1842.

[5] Letter to his sister, Sarah, dated 19th July 1842.

[6] Sarah Selwyn "Reminiscences" page 19.

[7] A clerical student who had come out from England with the Bishop's party.

[8] Letter to his sisters, Sarah and Phoebe - 10th January 1843.

[9] Journal Volume V page 56

[10] Ibid page 57.

[11] [Selwyn] Extracts from Letters - Allan K Davidson "Selwyn's Legacy" page 31.

[12] Extract from a letter of G A Selwyn -ibid page 31.

[13] G A Selwyn "New Zealand" Part I - ibid page 31

[14] Una Platts "The Lively Capital" page 107

[15] Allan K Davidson "Selwyn's Legacy" page 40.

[16] Mary Martin "Our Maoris" page 31.

[17] William Bambridge Diaries 17th March 1843

[18] Journal Volume IV page 106.

[19] Letter to his sister, Sarah, dated 15 April 1843.

[20] Warren E Limbrick (Editor) "Bishop Selwyn in New Zea;and 1841-1846" page 46.

[21] Allan K Davidson "Selwyn's Legacy" page 68.

[22] Ruth Etherington "William Charles Cotton" Auckland Waikato Historical Society

[23] Allan K Davidson "Selwyn's Legacy" page 34

[24] A G Bagnall & G C Petersen "William Colenso" Wellington NZ 1948 page 49.

[25] Letter from Elizabeth Colenso to Mrs A N Brown dated 30 August 1843 - quoted by A G Bagnall and G C Petersen "William Colenso" page 154.

[26] Bagnall and Petersen page 154.

[27] Letter to Mr Coleridge dated 28th October 1842.

[28] Letter to his sister, Phoebe 8th May 1843.

[29] Letter to his mother 30th May 1843.

[30] Letter to his sister, Sarah, dated 19th July 1843.

[31] Ibid 19th July 1843.

[32] Mary Martin "Our Maoris" page 23.

[33] Helen Hogan "Renata's Journey" page 45.

[34] Ibid page 65.

[35] Una Platts "The Lively Capital" page 104.

[36] Journal Volume VII page 22.

[37] Journal Volume VII page 24.

[38] Extracts from Cotton's letter published in the London Times 20th April 1843 and re-printed in the Auckland Chronicle 27th September 1843.

[39] Letter to his father dated 20th April 1843.

[40] Jane, and her husband William, were CMS missionaries to Poverty Bay. They lived at the Tauranga Mission House, Bay of Plenty.

[41] Allan K Davidson "Selwyn's Legacy" page 41.

[42] Letter to his sister, Phoebe, written at the Waimate on 8th May 1844.

CHAPTER FIVE

THE MOVE TO AUCKLAND

The Importance of Cotton's Role

We have seen how Selwyn had established St John's College at the Waimate in premises owned by the Church Missionary Society. In 1844 certain differences arose between the Bishop and the CMS, and the Society gave notice that they were unwilling to extend the lease. The decision was no great blow to the Bishop, as his plan had always been to reside there for a few years and then, as he said, "to sally forth." So he decided to move the College to Tamaki, near Kohimarama, Auckland, about 160 miles south of the Bay of Islands. He had bought about 450 acres of land there and he gave the area the name of Bishop's Auckland. Not wishing to be an unwelcome tenant on CMS land, he decided to carry out the move straight away.

On Monday 22nd September 1844 there was a large gathering of natives at the Waimate settlement. The Maori always came on Mondays to bring their produce to sell and everyone called it 'market day.' But first they had school and catechizing, and only after that did the trading begin. But many had heard rumours that the Bishop was leaving and they had come to express their sorrow and disappointment at his imminent departure. Some, no doubt, protested for the practical reason that they would be losing a valuable market for their produce. Others had grown to respect the Bishop and they would miss his teaching and care for them. However, when it was explained that in Auckland he would be nearer to the centre of his diocese, most accepted the wisdom of the move.

William Charles Cotton MA
1813 - 1879
Priest, Missionary and Bee Master

*The Bishop's House, with the carpenter's shop,
the printing office and the hospital to the right. October 1844. William Bambridge.
Journal Volume IX page vii. Dixson Library, State Library of New South Wales.*

After weeks of preparation, mainly spent in packing their belongings and equipment, the day of departure finally arrived. At 7 o'clock on the morning of 23rd October 1844, with no doubt considerable sadness, the Bishop, Mrs Selwyn and their two children left the Waimate. (Willie was five and Johnnie, the new baby, six months old). Mrs Selwyn and Willie, rode on horseback, whilst the Bishop travelled on foot, carrying his infant son. William Martin and his wife, Mary, followed them about an hour later, eight native bearers carrying Mrs Martin in a small litter. Friends came to bid them farewell and the Maori children sang "Oh that will be joyful........."

After a couple of weeks delay in Paihia, the Government Brig *"Victoria"* finally arrived and, shortly afterwards, the first party set sail. They reached Auckland on 17th November. Selwyn had decided to set up the new St John's College in temporary quarters at Purewa Creek, near Tamaki. The party encamped by a small woodland at the head of the creek. Years later Lady Martin described it as "a lovely spot, for the high banks were thickly wooded to the water's edge, and the rimu which droops like weeping willow, and the yellow kowai, abounded."[1] This provisional camp consisted mainly of tents, many of which had been donated by Cotton's father. A large tent,[2] in which they also slept and dined, served as a schoolhouse for the Maori boys, whilst the rest of the party were lodged in seven smaller tents.

During this period Cotton was extremely busy helping to ensure that the move ran smoothly and that everyone's possessions arrived without mishap. At the same time he was concerned for the welfare of his bees. As a temporary measure he settled them in Mrs Martin's garden at Taurarua in the adjoining Judges Bay. On Monday 18th November 1844 he recorded: "Got the whale boat (sic) over the side between six and seven. Sent some of the party ashore. Captain Bough lent me his six oared boat for the rest and for my bees, which have arrived quite safe and are working as merrily in Mrs M's garden as tho they had not travelled 160 miles."[3]

The following day he took the whaleboat out to the Government Brig and collected William Davies and all his Maori school boys to take them to the settlement. As they approached the creek the boys sang "Rule Britannia" and "Hearts of Oak" most lustily to the great astonishment of the pakehas watching on the shore.

On Wednesday 20th November WCC found he could not use the Government launch as, the previous day, she "had started a plank" when carrying stones to make a small pier in Commercial Bay. Instead he took the *Marian*, "rigged her for the occasion, and brought some things off in her." Clearly it was not only a busy day but, as his account shows, an anxious one with the difficulties of navigating the Purewa Creek: "Captain Porter's barge had started to the College with a load. And after taking two tremendous loads in the whale boat, of Mr Bambridge's things from the *Dolphin*, and so clearing her out, I followed in the barge, and it was well I did so, for had not we been with her to tow, she would not have got up to the warf (sic) in one tide."[4]

William Charles Cotton MA
1813 - 1879
Priest, Missionary and Bee Master

Bishop's Auckland - the temporary establishment of St John's College, Purewa, three miles from Auckland, July 1845, showing the church tent and other buildings. Caroline Harriet(Palmer) Abraham. Ink on paper. A-128-005. Alexander Turnbull Library, Wellington, New Zealand.

Bringing goods ashore at Purewa. Cotton (wearing the cap) helping a work party carry the main body of Mr Fisher's dray. Thomas Biddulph Hutton. Pencil. Journal Volume VIII page 6. Dixson Library, State Library of New South Wales.

William Charles Cotton MA
1813 - 1879
Priest, Missionary and Bee Master

In the meantime Bishop Selwyn had rented a large house nearby in Parnell for himself, Mrs Selwyn and the boys. Cotton arranged for the Bishop's goods to be taken by horse and dray up the steep hill to the house for two shillings a load,[5] thanks to an agreement he negotiated with a local carter. At this stage most of the party continued to sleep in the Brig, but Cotton stayed at the Reverend Mr Churton's cottage,[6] sleeping outside in a tent, as he said, preferring "the feel of the fern to any mattress." On Monday 25th November he was busy all day helping to pitch the Great Tent and to set up the Stanhope press. As one might expect there were hazards in this work and at one point in the latter job he got a terrible pinch.

In the ensuing weeks he was constantly sailing one or other of the boats on various missions - one day landing parties of people, on another day bringing goods ashore or visiting the stores in Auckland. On one occasion he sailed up the coast to Matakana with colleagues and a party of masons to see if the stone there was suitable for facings. Undoubtedly during this period the Bishop was pleased that Cotton took charge so decisively and supervised the settling in at Purewa. This enabled Selwyn, in due course, to leave with an easy mind on his third episcopal visitation.

During his brief stay in Purewa, Selwyn had held divine worship for the local Orakei and Okahu Maori. He planned that when he left these services were to be taken by his chaplain alternately at Tamaki and at their own settlements. On Sunday 8th December it was Purewa's first turn. About 9 o'clock the Maori started to come in and various classes and services were held, ending with evening worship in the "Great Tent."

The following Sunday Frederic Fisher arrived in Hobson's Bay on the *Nimrod*. On board were 24 head of cattle that he had brought from the Waimate. Cotton welcomed him to Bishop's Auckland and made the necessary arrangements for the cattle to be taken out to the Purewa settlement.

Soon it became one of WCC's main duties to take the services in the little church of St Thomas at Tamaki. Of recent construction, this church had been built of scoria (volcanic stone) and covered with soft facings which rapidly began to deteriorate. Although Cotton thought it had a venerable appearance, it was to last only twenty years. However, until the College chapel was built, it served the needs of the Purewa settlement and the local farmers' families. The inaugural service at the new church had been a memorable occasion. Reverend WC Dudley wrote: "It was a most appropriate day for the opening, the first stone having been laid on this day last year. The Maori boys sang the 100th Psalm. I have not seen such an English sight or been so moved since I have been in the Colony. It made my eyes tearful, and my voice husky......"[7]

Later in December, the young men at the College decided, no doubt with Cotton's encouragement, to hold a grand dinner on Christmas Day. Invitations were sent out to both pakehas and Maori, with the invitations in Maori printed on the College press. The dinner was to be held in the Great Tent with a table laid for about twenty pakeha and twenty Maori special guests. In readiness the Tent and St Thomas's Church were decorated with colourful wild flowers. Unfortunately for the organizers, perhaps through lack of proper planning, a number of problems arose with the arrangements. On Christmas morning Cotton was busy taking services in the Great Tent and then at St Thomas's. When he returned he found the impatient for their dinner. As he hardly knew the people of Orakei and Okahu he had difficulty in finding the principal chiefs to ask them to take their places at the table. Consequently some Maori leaders were upset and one, Roto Waitea, who had been a friend of the Bishop's and Mrs Selwyn's 'steward' at Parnell, wrote a critical account of the event. One passage read: "great was the wrath of the people who sat without - they went away like a routed army."[8]

William Charles Cotton MA
1813 - 1879
Priest, Missionary and Bee Master

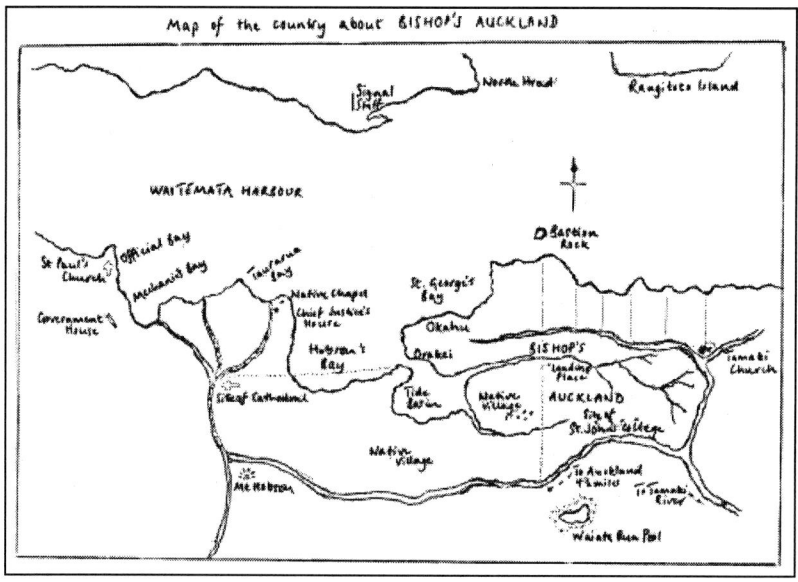

Map and plan of the country about Bishop's Auckland. Pen and ink.
William Bambridge Journal Volume IX page viii.
Dixson Library, State Library of New South Wales.

After all the hard work of establishing the settlement at Purewa, everyone must have felt the need for some relaxation. No doubt they enjoyed a number of social gatherings. One such occasion was their celebration of Twelfth Night when WCC organized a special party. After taking the service (in Maori) at Tamaki, he rowed the whaleboat to Taurarua and brought Mrs Smith,[9] Sarah and Catherine Williams and the Misses Davies over to the settlement. With a few other guests, including some neighbours, they enjoyed a pleasant evening together. They started with tea in the Great Tent which was splendidly illuminated with "three extempore chandeliers." After tea they played round games, danced and then concluded with a boisterous session of snapdragon where the guests tried to pluck raisins out of burning brandy. "I had three separate sets of snapdragon," wrote Cotton, "one for ourselves, one for the Maori boys, who are capital hands at it, and the other for the Maori men. Brandy and salt was then in requisition, and oh such a set of countenances, with the bright black eyes of the Maori boys peering out from the darkness visible. They raised a tremendous shout every time the flames leapt up as I stirred the mixture with a stick."[10] Clearly Cotton played an important role in arranging and hosting these social gatherings and enjoyed the responsibility placed upon him.

One night, towards the end of January 1845, they had a terrible storm and Cotton wrote that he was "in a puddle all night" and his blankets were completely soaked. "Such howling of the wind I never heard, even at sea. The Maori boys all ran out of the great tent, expecting it would fall, and it was only saved by the careful way we pitched it, and the strength of the weather lines, three of which were to the Eastward, from which quarter the wind came." He was much relieved when morning came and he could go to the store for some dry clothes. After this experience he hoped that some raupo houses would soon be erected for them. These were temporary buildings, with wooden frames, where the roof and walls were made of rushes.

A Valuable Contribution

As mentioned earlier, WCC had decided to accompany Selwyn to New Zealand without the blessing of his father and he remained under an obligation to return within five years. Throughout his first few years at the Waimate he was constantly hoping for his father's approbation. One feels that he was almost straining every nerve and sinew to serve the Bishop well so that his father would be pleased with Selwyn's commendations. Commenting on his willingness to become headmaster of the Collegiate School, he wrote "I am glad to be able practically to shew the Bishop that my readiness to do any thing he sets me to do, is not mere talk. And he feels it so, too. I hope the letters both he and Mrs Selwyn sent have reached home safe. I long to have under Papa's own hand that he is satisfied with the step I have taken........"[11]

At the same time he invited Selwyn to send his best wishes to his mother. It must have given Cotton immense delight to find that the Bishop had written the following message:

"Many happy returns of May 29th 1843. Our first year concluded with many reasons for thankfulness, not the least the zealous and effective friendship, and sound discretion of W.C.C." He clearly thought that this was one of the best character references that anyone could have given him.

Writing to Cotton's father some two years later, Selwyn made these remarks about his son's character: "I really believe that William is very much beloved by many of those who might have been expected to look upon him and his principles with distrust"[12] Undoubtedly this was a reference to Cotton's (along with Selwyn's) High Church beliefs, with which the CMS missionaries generally disagreed. Selwyn added that his chaplain's general affability and readiness to help everyone had been greatly appreciated by the Church Mission Clergy.

In another passage in this letter Selwyn referred to Cotton's long-standing problem with over-spending. He called it "William's monomania with spending." He explained how the poverty of the colony and the threat to trade posed by the native disturbances meant that many of the parents of the boys in the English School were unable to pay their fees. As a result the Bishop had decided that the only way to keep the school open was for the boys to spend more time in some useful occupation, such as growing fruit and vegetables or helping to look after livestock. All this Selwyn argued "struck at the roots of William's monomania with spending, as I exercise the tyranny of a Dragon over every unnecessary expenditure, as if every pound were the fruits of the Hesperides." Selwyn explained that he and Cotton had had a few "gentle altercations about spending," but, with the financial difficulties that faced the mission, Cotton saw the need for restraint and careful management of his money.

William Charles Cotton MA
1813 - 1879
Priest, Missionary and Bee Master

The Problem of Finance

By June 1845 there were about fifty pupils boarding at the pakeha and Maori schools. Cotton thought that the native school could be greatly expanded. In fact he argued such provision had to be made at St John's College and similar institutions, if the Maori were to survive as a race. The main problem was finance and it became a great worry for the Bishop. Besides difficulties arising from parents being unable to pay their children's fees, there were problems with other sources of funds. Grants from the Society for the Propagation of the Gospel and the Church Missionary Society had become very precarious. The CMS gave £600 - 00 a year and hoped that the investment of some of this money in land would eventually bring them a return that would relieve them of the burden of these annual payments. But Cotton had grave doubts. He thought that these investments would never produce one tenth of the amount expected. The third source of income for St John's came from Parliament, but this grant had to be approved each year. The College faced the serious risk that one day Parliament might not give its approval.

Because of the uncertain state of their funding, the Bishop had resolved to try to make the College even more self-supporting. Soon all were lending a hand, including the schoolboys. However many people were unsympathetic to the establishment of such an academic institution in the primitive conditions in which they lived. Remarks made by Colonel Hulme of the *North Star* were typical of many visitors to Bishop's Auckland. He had been sent in 1845 to assist the Governor in the suppression of the Maori uprising in the north. Before he came to Purewa, he scoffed at the idea of such a College. "Latin and Greek" he exclaimed, "what is the use of teaching that? Let them all leave to bear arms." But when he arrived and saw the boys hard at work in the fields, he changed his mind. He had quickly recognized the valuable contribution that the school was making to the community.

William Charles Cotton MA
1813 - 1879
Priest, Missionary and Bee Master

After the Wairau massacre[13] in 1843 relations between the white settlers and the Maori deteriorated in some parts of New Zealand. In 1845 trouble flared up in the Bay of Islands, "where," Cotton says, "we were so quietly settled a year ago." A party of natives, led by John Heke, cut down the flagstaff at Kororareka. Troops were hastily brought over from Sydney, and with their help, it was replaced. But again the natives rose up in protest and, for a second time, they cut the flagstaff down. Once more it was re-erected and a guardhouse established. In March 1845 it was attacked again and many shots were fired. The natives hid in the surrounding brushwood, firing intermittently. Soldiers were summoned from a sloop in the bay and, in the skirmish which followed, their commander was mortally wounded and his men driven away. Then, for the third time, the flagstaff was cut down. Eventually more troops were brought in and law and order restored, but not without the destruction of Kororareka and some loss of life.

The underlying causes of the rebellion seem to have been grievances over the ownership of land and a decline in trade. Sadly these events marked the beginning of a long period of often violent struggle between the Maori and the pakehas in some districts of New Zealand. During these troubles Bishop Selwyn spent much of his time preaching peace and tolerance and trying to resolve the differences between the two sides.

In the meantime the Bishop's party were living peacefully with their Maori friends at Purewa. In fact they had just successfully completed building the last of the temporary raupo huts. In a letter to his sisters Cotton wrote: "Our houses are all up and watertight now that the bad weather is coming on. You could hardly think that any think (sic) could be built so comfortable mainly of rushes as that in which I am now sitting."

William Charles Cotton MA
1813 - 1879
Priest, Missionary and Bee Master

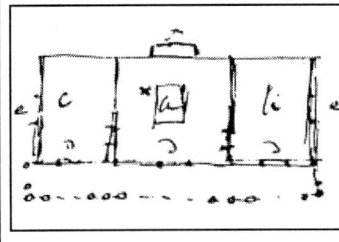

In the same letter he made the above sketch and plan of the small house in which he and Frederic Fisher were living, and gave the details quoted below:

a. The sitting room
b. The first bedroom which Mrs Selwyn is to occupy.
c. Mr Fisher's room
d. Three french windows, so that each house has a door on to the verandah.
e. Two casement windows with lead lights.
f. The fireplace.
x. "The spot at which I am now sitting - Fisher is at the other side of the table making odd remarks about a book on agriculture which he is reading.
The verandah is supported by Kauri poles, which will look very nice when covered with creepers."[14]

The room, which he calls the first bedroom, had canvas stretched between the principal uprights of the house. Then the canvas had been covered in wallpaper. The ceiling had calico stretched very tightly across it. All this, Cotton says, made the room very snug. Finally, he added, "I have been hard at work turning the posts of a French bedsted (sic) which I hope to have up on Monday and then the sooner she (Mrs Selwyn) comes the better."

William Charles Cotton MA
1813 - 1879
Priest, Missionary and Bee Master

He had first discovered the parts of a "very excellent" lathe, made by Holtzkaphelt, when rooting about in the stores at the Waimate towards the end of April 1843. Despite its poor condition he persuaded the Bishop to buy it from the CMS, and then he cleaned and assembled it. However almost all the tools and the chucks were missing and so a few weeks later he wrote to his sister, Sarah, to arrange for a check to be made with the manufacturers whether the parts from his old lathe had the same screw. If that were so, then, provided his brothers, Henry and Arthur, did not wish to use the lathe, the parts could be sent out to him. Although it is difficult to be certain, probably it was this lathe that he was operating in June 1845.

After his description of the raupo house, Cotton gives us a brief glimpse of one or two other aspects of his life at Purewa. He mentions that he had been down for evening Prayers to the schoolhouse[15] where all the pakehas of the College assemble. "The Maori boys and servants have their service in the Native schoolroom. Samuel Williams, the master of the boys, is the Kai Karakia, as a missionary report would say, conducts their devotions." After the service he had his supper which consisted of a large bowl of oatmeal porridge made by Mrs Prince, the College bed maker.

One way in which John Heke's rebellion did affect St John's College was that, as Mrs Selwyn declared: "in good hearted pity for the Korereka (sic) sufferers," Cotton invited a large number of the indigenous scholars of that town to come over free to the school in Auckland. Unfortunately this proved embarrassing for the Bishop as he had to provide for far more pupils than he could afford and caused some ill feeling among the parents of the original pupils. However in the next few months staff and scholars undertook more self-supporting work and slowly the College finances improved.

William Charles Cotton MA
1813 - 1879
Priest, Missionary and Bee Master

St John's College at Purewa 1845. William Bambridge.
Pen and wash on coloured paper.

1. Kitchen 2. Dining Hall & Printing Office. 3. Farmer's House. 4. Reverend Cotton's and Mr Fisher's. 5. Mr Bambridge's 6. Mr Telford (the printer). 7. Vacancy. House taken to new site. 8. Carpenter's Shop 9. Laundress and Captain of Schooner 10. Laundress and Butler. 11. Barn used as schools. 12. Native Master's and Scholars. 13. House for Native Visitors. 14. Potato Store.

The first six months of 1845 had been a busy time for Cotton. Selwyn had been away for much of the time and the whole business of managing the new settlement had fallen on his shoulders. He stated that the schools were running well with Mr Samuel Williams in charge of the Maori School and Mr Tudor and Mr Hutton looking after the English Boys' School. On 6th June he wrote that the Bishop wished him to remain in New Zealand a little beyond his five years apprenticeship which meant he would be returning home towards the end of 1847. At the same time Selwyn would be sending his son, Willie, to England under WCC's "parental care."

New Buildings for St John's

Once the College was established in its temporary accommodation at Purewa, work could start on the construction of a permanent headquarters. A small committee consisting of the Bishop, the Chief Justice, the Attorney General and Mr Kempthorne, the architect, had already chosen site. Gradually over the course of the next twelve months a number of buildings were erected, including the College hall, the chapel and even a hospital, but not without some severe difficulties. As John Evans explains: "The contractors failed owing to the depressed state of the country and government spending raised prices. On the desertion of the stonemasons, the idea of completing the college in stone had to be given up, and the completion in wood was greatly hampered by the high wages of the carpenters. All this did not deter Selwyn, who went with parties of boys in the *Flying Fish* to buy timber from the neighbouring islands, and by May 1846 the main part of the college establishment had been transferred."[16]

Lady Martin stated that, though the site was a healthy one, the grey scoria buildings stood out on the bleak higher ground above the creek, and their appearance was not so picturesque. Nevertheless the Bishop, she explained, saw great possibilities in the situation for landscape gardening. She wrote later: "The ground sloped through a wooded glen, full of tree ferns, to the sea. He had winding paths cut, and the lads made flower beds, and planted fruit trees and flowering shrubs in the hollow. Every year saw some improvement."[17]

Visit to Taranaki

Over the years Cotton had become a good friend of Mr and Mrs Bolland, who ran the Taranaki Mission. In August 1845 William Bolland, who had been made deacon two years before, came to Auckland to be ordained. Selwyn had asked WCC to take care of the mission station for six weeks whilst he was away. On 9th August Cotton set out on foot to make the journey to Taranaki. It is perhaps an indication of the affection in which WCC was held that the whole school and some of the College students accompanied him on the first leg of the journey. After a while they gradually dropped away and returned home. The last to leave were Messrs Judd and Dale who went with him as far as the Parakua woods where they dined. Then, laden with "Supple Jack" (branches like willows for basket-making), they turned back and left him to go on alone.

Although Cotton enjoyed the walk, he found it hard going at times. As it was winter the days were short, cold and often wet, and he had to endure considerable hardship, especially when crossing flooded rivers. Some days he became extremely tired and hungry. But eventually he reached his destination and his good spirits were quickly restored by Mrs Bolland's hearty welcome.

On his arrival he was pleased to find the house much improved since his last visit. The roof, which had been torn off in a gale six months before, had been replaced and thatched. There were two churches in the district and he found **"a nice attentive congregation"** at both of them. As he had expected, his stay at Taranaki turned out to be a pleasant change from the usual routine of St John's College.

Mary Eliza Hawkins

In August 1846 Cotton received a final shattering piece of news - Eliza had decided to marry another man. He stated in a letter to his sister, Phoebe, that he was determined not to be despondent. He explained that in his prayers over the last few years on the many occasions when his thoughts had turned to Eliza, he had prayed for a favourable response from her. But he always added the plea that if it should not happen then God grant him the strength to withstand the blow. "So I have always added to my prayer for her ....a supplication that I might have grace to submit with cheerfulness, if it was not to be, and I now feel that my prayer is answered."[18]

When he showed the letters to Mrs Selwyn, she read them without comment and then gave him a motherly hug and said "God comfort you, my son, and give you peace. I can do nothing but pray for you." Cotton concluded his letter with the statement that though "one deep rooted hope has been torn up," he would continue to carry out his duties in the usual way. He hoped that the happiness he expected Eliza to find with him, she would now discover with another man. With these words he seems to suggest that he could cope with his bitter disappointment. But probably this rejection left him with a wound which took many years to heal, and then maybe never completely.

At about this time Phoebe also felt sad and bereft. Earlier in the year her sister, Sarah, had married Henry Acland and had gone to live in Oxford. Phoebe and Sarah had always had a close relationship and now she felt the loss of her sister's daily companionship.

The Fever Epidemic

Shortly after their arrival at Purewa Creek the Bishop had established a small hospital similar to the one at the Waimate. By May 1846 many of the pupils and students had moved into the new College buildings and in September Selwyn announced the opening of a new hospital. It was housed in a wooden building constructed on scoria foundations. It had several rooms, including separate men's and women's wards.

Sadly, in March 1847, fever broke out at the hospital. Both of the Selwyn's children, Willie and Johnnie, caught it and the former became extremely ill. Cotton wrote: "Willie seemed almost beyond hope.......... he screamed almost incessantly for ten days, rolling his head from side to side.........." WCC played a full part in looking after the sick, giving up his room to accommodate the doctor and his wife who had both caught the fever. In the meantime he slept in the schoolhouse so as to be on hand to look after the boys, sharing the nursing of three sick boys with Samuel Williams, the schoolmaster. In a letter to his brother, Henry, in May 1847 he described how they desperately felt the need for better accommodation during the sickness. The situation had not been helped by the way the Maori schools were crowded into one wing of the hospital building. It was a miracle that none of the pupils contracted the fever. He explained that during the epidemic he had little time to spare, and when he did have, he felt too distressed to write any letters. In total there were about thirty people who went down with the fever and, tragically, two of them died.

*A panoramic view of St John's College, Auckland
by Caroline Abraham lithographed by Miss Cotton and published in Auckland 1862.
(Alexander Turnbull Library).
The buildings from left to right were: the printing office, the washhouse, the Bishop's House, the Hall, the English School and the kitchen. In the other house on the right were: the Maori Adult School, the weaving room and the surgery.*

The Bee Master

The dispatch of the bees promised by friends in New South Wales took much longer than Cotton had expected. It was not until his friend, James Busby, visited Sydney in May 1843 that an opportunity arose for some hives to be shipped back with him. On his return two months later he brought back three hives supplied by Mrs Sparke and Reverend Dr Thomas Steele of Cook's River. Of these only one hive, called "The Queen," survived and this was kept in Busby's garden in Waitangi. The first swarm from this hive, "The Princess Royal," was given to WCC in March 1844 as well as later ones, called the Princesses "Mary" and "Alice."

Cotton had waited seven months for any of the 'Busby' bees to be brought over to the Waimate. After losing a swarm that arrived on Tuesday 5th March, he tried again on the 12th. This time he managed to hive the bees successfully. "The Bees this morning were bringing in great loads of a very red pollen" he recorded. "I have all my life desired to have such a summer house, and now I come to New Zealand and find it."[19] At long last he had acquired some bees and he could start the pleasant task of building up an apiary of his own.

When Selwyn decided to transfer St John's College to Bishop's Auckland, Cotton had to move his bees again. This time he succeeded in transporting his hives from the Waimate to Purewa Creek - a distance of some 160 miles - without any harm befalling them.

Cotton's raupo house at Purewa Creek, 1845. Note the apiary to the rear. Journal Volume VII. Dixson Library, State Library of New South Wales.

Throughout this time until he left New Zealand, Cotton was busy helping and advising settlers and Maori in the best practices of keeping bees and gathering honey. One day, a few weeks after his arrival in Kohimarama, he was enjoying "a capital sail" in the *Marian*, when it

William Charles Cotton MA
1813 - 1879
Priest, Missionary and Bee Master

started to rain so heavily, that he decided to land at Captain Bough's house in Official Bay. His arrival was opportune. The Captain was in the garden trying to hive a swarm of bees. Cotton, though dripping wet, hurried over to help with the task. But first, he asked for some warm wine and water, which Mrs Bough gladly prepared, thinking to his amusement, that it was for the bees, not for the bee-master!

Just as Cotton believed that the poor cottagers in England gained by bee keeping, so he was convinced that the Maori would do so, too. As they were highly skilled in making baskets and mats, they would soon learn the art of making straw skeps. In a similar way, when a swarm landed in the high branches, the Maori were adept at climbing the tree and collecting the bees, often in a cloth or a shirt or, in one case, a pair of trousers. Here are a few examples of Cotton's bee-keeping activities with the native people. On Saturday 9th January 1847, he wrote "walked inland to see the Bee House which the Maori have put up here for their Bees."[20] Thursday 14th January: "Taught three Maori to make straw hives. I just know the stitch well enough to put others in the way of it, but I was soon surprised by my Maori pupils. Returned home by way of Martin's Bee kainga - the new swarms are doing very well."[21] Incidentally, as the Maori had never seen honeybees before they were introduced in 1839, they called them "the whiteman's fly."

Towards the end of 1844 Cotton published "A Few Simple Rules for New Zealand Beekeepers," in which he gave a lot of sound advice on the best ways to look after bees and how and when to remove the honey. At the same time he repeated his plea that all beekeepers should adopt more humane ways of taking the honey from the hive than the old sulphur-pit method. As explained earlier, Cotton wanted beekeepers simply to drive the bees from one box to another by blowing smoke at them and then the honey could be removed without harming the bees.

In 1847, in response to a number of requests, he wrote a series of articles for *"The New Zealander"* under the title "Hints on Bee Management."[22] He then decided to use these articles as the basis for a book. He only completed the text shortly before his departure, so he left instructions with a friend to arrange for its publication. The book was printed at The Spectator Office, Manners Street, Wellington in 1848 under the title "A Manual for New Zealand Beekeepers." Clearly Cotton saw the need for such a work because he realized that New Zealand was a good country for bees and that many of the settlers were new to beekeeping and its techniques.

The pages are full of sound advice on the best practical ways of keeping bees and producing good quality honey. The topics covered include: the best situation for an apiary, different types of hives, taking honey, preparing honey and wax for sale and the enemies of bees. Before the introduction of honeybees, the colonists had to send over to England every year for white clover seed, as it did not seed freely there. A year later the St John's Press published another of his books on the art of beekeeping. This one, "Ko nga pi" (The Bees), he had written in Maori, to give the indigenous population the same opportunity to profit from his advice.

Letters

Throughout his stay in New Zealand Cotton corresponded regularly with members of his family. Most of these letters were addressed to Walwood House, Leytonstone, Essex. He always wrote separately to his mother and father. About once a month he sent a letter to his sister, Agnes, but more frequently to his sisters, Sarah and Phoebe. He corresponded much less often with his brothers, Henry and Arthur Benjamin. In all these letters he showed his love and affection for his family, and especially for his two older sisters.

In the manner of a well-educated Victorian gentleman, he corresponded with his family and friends at great length. Some of his letters ran to six or more pages. He must have spent a large part of his day, or more likely his evening, working on his correspondence. Approximately 150 of his New Zealand letters have survived and are now preserved in the Selwyn College Archives in Cambridge.

Farewell to New Zealand

By the summer of 1846 Cotton had decided that he would visit his family in England and then return to his work at St John's College. It is not clear how he had evaded the commitment made to his father to return home within five years. In a number of letters in July and August 1846 he stated that he intended to set sail in October, November or December of the following year. The exact date depended on when a direct sailing became available. He expected that Willie would be coming to England with him and, as he wrote to his sister, Sarah, the boy would be "under my Parental care."

Mrs Selwyn stated in her memoirs that, without doubt, he wanted to return to New Zealand. She wrote: "In this year (1847), though not till December, Mr Cotton left us for England, fully intending to return, I think - but illness at home put an end to this, and he never came back."[23]

Arrangements were soon made for his voyage home and by early December the time had come for Cotton to leave St John's College. On Wednesday 8th December everyone gathered in the chapel for a service to mark his imminent departure. Worship began with the reading of the lessons, and then he recited a few special prayers, including a collect for St John's College which he used for the first time. After he had chanted the Litany, he gave his farewell address, on the theme of obedience, unity and brotherly love. Finally he called the boys up one at a time and gave each of them a hearty handshake and presented them with a small Prayer Book in which he had inscribed the pupil's name. He showed how moved he had been by the occasion when he wrote later: "My voice trembled when I began the service, but by the third petition it had quite recovered its tone."

At this point the Bishop rose from his seat and, with Cotton kneeling at his feet, placed his hands on his chaplain's head, and gave him his blessing, concluding with the words "Go in peace and the Lord be with thee."[23] Cotton was very moved by this but the Bishop's words helped to assuage the sorrow he felt at the prospect of leaving. He wrote later: "the bitterness of parting was over. I did not shed another tear all day." But, according to Sarah Selwyn, plenty of other tears were flowing: "The conclusion was overpowering, the poor boys restrained their feelings till Cotton knelt down to receive a blessing ....when they simultaneously burst into tears, which continued to flow till they left the Chapel."

In the afternoon the Bishop gave him a prayer book with the inscription "W.C.C. a parting gift from his grateful and affectionate friend G.A.S. (& S.H.S.) in remembrance of seven years of friendship by land and sea." Later in the day he said a final good-bye to Mrs Selwyn. He described his feelings in these words:
"All was finished and I said my last goodbye. It was too much for tears, indeed the bitterness of parting was over, when on the day of the consecration I administered the H.C. (Holy Communion) to Mrs Selwyn, and yet I returned two or three times for another embrace, God grant it may not (be) a final one, and at last with an effort and a 'gulp,' fairly ran out of the room, closing the door after me."[24]

Later, riding his pony, *"General"*, Cotton called on his many friends to bid them farewell, including the Attorney General and the Governor. "At last I said farewell and trust I may find both the Governor and Mrs Grey in Auckland at my return, should God spare me............"
Once again we see that he had every intention of returning to New Zealand in the near future and carrying on his work with Bishop Selwyn. In the evening, after many sad partings, he and Mr & Mrs Bambridge and their children, embarked on the *Deborah* and prepared themselves for the voyage to Sydney.

William Charles Cotton MA
1813 - 1879
Priest, Missionary and Bee Master

From the evidence of his final letters home, he appears to have left New Zealand in good spirits. In one letter he explained how Fisher, Hutton and Purchas had been ordained deacons for service at St John's College and that the various offices which he held would be divided between them during his absence.[25] In correspondence with his sister, Phoebe, he mentioned that he would have preferred to return via Hong Kong in order to see something of China, India and Egypt. But he was obliged to take a passage from Sydney on the "Penyard Park" which he feared might be "4 months of imprisonment." Nevertheless he expressed his determination to find some profitable employment on board. He was already committed to helping look after the Slack and Bambridge children, ten of them in all, by supervising lessons given by William Bambridge. Also he would be reading with Leonard Williams who, as the first student of St John's College to gain a place at Oxford, was sailing to England with them.[26] From the tone of these letters one gets the impression that, though he was extremely sad to leave New Zealand, he intended to make the most of his voyage home.

NOTES AND REFERENCES - CHAPTER FIVE

[1] Mary Martin "Our Maoris" page 62

[2] The large tent had previously gone with the Bishop on his travels but now he had decided it would be more useful at Purewa.

[3] Journal Volume VII page 192.

[4] Journal Volume VII page 196.

[5] Journal Volume VII page 24.

[6] Mr Churton had offered the use of his recently built, small brick house at St George's Bay.

[7] Letter to WCC from Reverend WC Dudley 7th January 1845.

[8] Una Platts "The Lively Capital" page 118.

[9] Mrs Elizabeth Smith had been a member of the Bishop's advance party that came over from Sydney in the Bristolian. She became a companion and housekeeper to Mrs Martin, who often suffered from poor health.

[10] Journal Volume IX page 17.

[11] Letter to his mother 30th May 1843, sending his birthday wishes.

[12] Selwyn's letter to William Cotton (senior) 23rd May 1845.

[13] Following the signing of the Treaty of Waitangi in 1840, it was not long before the weaknesses of the settlement and ineffective enforcement led to fierce clashes over land. In 1843 fighting broke

out in the Wairau Valley, near Blenheim. When settlers from the New Zealand Company started to survey disputed land, the Maori chiefs burned the survey huts and then fought with an armed party sent after them, killing twenty-two men.

[14] Letter to his sisters dated 9 June 1845.

[15] According to Mrs Selwyn, the great barn served as a schoolroom and hall - see Sarah Selwyn "Reminiscences" page 27.

[16] John H Evans "Churchman Militant" page 108.

[17] Mary Martin "Our Maoris" page 62/63

[18] Letter to Phoebe 5th August 1846.

[19] Journal Volume VII page 15.

[20] Journal Volume XI page 162.

[21] Journal Volume XI page 167.

[22] Peter Barrett "William Charles Cotton – Grand Bee Master of New Zealand"
page 123.

[23] Sarah Selwyn "Reminiscences" page 32.

[24] Journal Volume XII page 2.

[25] Letter to his brother, Arthur Benjamin, dated 27th November 1847.

[26] Letter to his sister, Phoebe, dated 29th November 1847.

CHAPTER SIX

RETURN TO ENGLAND

On his return to England in May 1848 Cotton had a number of serious problems to overcome. In the first place he would have to face his father. He had left England in 1841 under a paternal obligation to "prove himself and return within four years." In effect he had stayed six years and now he had resolved to return to New Zealand, a plan with which his father was unlikely to agree. Furthermore he had left these shores in the expectation that on his homecoming he would marry Mary Eliza Hawkins. Cotton had fallen in love with her and had left England in the belief that the feeling was mutual. In the middle of his stay in New Zealand his sisters began to hint in their letters that the marriage was unlikely. In May 1844 he heard the news that she was unwilling to continue her friendship with him.

However for the next couple of years he lived in the hope that she would change her mind, especially when the Bishop and Mrs Selwyn sent home good reports of him. As he stated himself his days of madness were all over and no judge or archbishop could have been a more grave or reverend suitor. But all the Selwyns's efforts on his behalf were to no avail. Finally, in August 1846, unbeknown to his friends in New Zealand, he learned the distressing news that Eliza had transferred her affections elsewhere. Without a doubt he found this loss hard to bear. The distress it caused probably affected him, on and off, for the rest of his life.

William Charles Cotton MA
1813 - 1879
Priest, Missionary and Bee Master

During his stay in New Zealand Cotton had coped well with his responsibilities. With the death of Reverend Whytehead, he had become the headmaster of the Collegiate School, as well as attending to numerous other duties, including helping to supervise the move to Auckland. Ruth Etherington states: "In fact he was the genial friend and helper to all in need and prime organizer of morale-raising parties. Occasions like Christmas and Twelfth Night provided welcome and necessary relaxation from an arduous life and the participants found they had not forgotten how to enjoy themselves."[1]

Clearly Cotton played a significant part in the life of the mission at the Waimate and later at Bishop's Auckland. But the thought of leaving the Selwyns and all his other companions must have been a depressing prospect, even though at this stage he was hoping to return. In addition he must have been conscious that he was giving up a settled and purposeful life in New Zealand, for an uncertain future in England.

Cotton left Auckland on 8th December 1847. Accompanying him was the schoolmaster, William Bambridge and his wife and their two children. They departed in the schooner *Deborah*, reaching Sydney thirteen days later, soon to board the sailing ship *Penyard Park* for home. They arrived in Penzance on 18th May 1848.

The Lost Years

The next nine years of Cotton's life - until he became the vicar of Frodsham - remain something of a mystery. There is no evidence of what transpired at his first meeting with his father and not a great deal is known of their subsequent relationship. However, as he never returned to New Zealand, one can only assume that his father refused to countenance such a proposal. Without his financial support, WCC did not have the means to return to Bishop's Auckland. It was probably this thwarting of his plans, in addition to the hurt caused by his rejection by Miss Hawkins, which brought on his severe depression. Some evidence for this is contained in one of Mrs Selwyn's letters to her friend, Reverend Coleridge. In November 1848 she wrote to him expressing great concern at reports of Cotton's ill health:

"The news of his arrival and illness has just reached us, and at first both because of its nature and extent, it was a great shock to us ....
The news reached us at Taurarua where it was felt deeply also but perhaps you will wonder to find that after time given and talking it over we all agreed in being much more hopeful about him and I trust that his improvement in health has justified this more favourable view. I do not mean that we doubted the presence of real illness when you wrote, but I hope that the surprise and pain his demeanour must have caused did not arise from the existence of so fearful a malady as seems to have been anticipated."[2]

Later in her letter Mrs Selwyn suggests that his friends may have got a false impression of him because they had forgotten his "free remarkable manner" and not realized that, in addition, he now showed a "peculiar colonial abandon in all matters of dress and deportment." Yet although Mrs Selwyn makes these allowances for his behaviour, she does agree that both she and Mrs Martin had seen signs of similar infirmity before he left New Zealand.

She went on to hope that WCC would be kept quiet, prevented from rushing about too much and given a suitable diet. But unfortunately there was no such simple set of remedies for Cotton's mental troubles. The several harsh blows he had been dealt must have had a devastating effect on his state of mind and probably he spent the next few years trying to overcome feelings of despondency.

There is further evidence of Cotton's illness in a letter from the Bishop dated 9th July 1849. Selwyn wrote at length giving him the latest news about St John's College, including a description of the new Hall. Then he stated how concerned he was to hear of his ill health and, in particular, of the "inflammation" from which he had suffered and hoped that it had not occurred again. Then he added the telling remark that he hoped that "this attack had not been as sharp as the one he had at the College before he left for England." Clearly Cotton had not enjoyed such good health in the months before his departure from New Zealand as we might be led to imagine by his letters and by the busy life he seemed to be leading.

Student of Christ Church

One of the few things, which is well established about WCC in this period of his life, is that he remained a Student of Christ Church, Oxford. "Student" meant "Fellow," a position which he had enjoyed for a number of years and for which he received an annual emolument. However, during the next nine years, he was in residence at the College only intermittently, his rooms being sub-let, and his sisters, Sarah and Phoebe, paying his dues.

It would appear from the scanty evidence available that he spent some time during these years travelling on the Continent. In 1853, for example, his father arranged for a Dr Arledge to join him at Rennes. The doctor was appointed not only to be Cotton's companion but also to organize his itinerary and to look after his financial affairs. His father told him that he had made these arrangements "to relieve you from the pecuniary difficulties in which we knew you were likely to be involved."[3]

William Charles Cotton MA
1813 - 1879
Priest, Missionary and Bee Master

Evidently he was still having problems managing his money in a responsible way.

At the time his father and mother were staying at a hotel in Bournemouth to help Mrs Cotton's recovery from a serious illness. From there on 1st March 1853 William Cotton wrote as follows: "I shall not regret the extra expense of your journeys if it has tended to your health and amusement and to enable you to acquire that self control which is so essential." Unfortunately Cotton did not enjoy Dr Arledge's company for very long and his father remarked that now he would have to find his own companions on his travels. Once again William Cotton was concerned about his son's inability to manage money. His bank account was overdrawn by £300 to £400, even after his studentship money had been paid in and his father had paid various expenses. Finally he exhorted his son not to let his expenses exceed £20 per day. William Cotton concluded his letter with the remark "If we knew where you are likely to be found, we could come to you" which suggests that his relationship with his son was decidedly strained and that WCC wished to have time on his own.

A further indication that Cotton was spending considerable time travelling is given in the Christ Church Chapter Book. An entry dated 23rd December 1854 states:
"A Medical Report having been received as to the health of Mr Cotton and it appearing that it is essential to his recovery that he should be allowed to travel in foreign parts, permission is given him to be absent for one year."[4]

Having gained his leave of absence from the College, he set out on a Continental tour early in 1855. By June of that year he had reached Constantinople, where he stayed as a guest of Lord Napier, the Chief Secretary to the British Embassy in that city. As usual the Ambassador and his suite were spending the summer at Therapia, where Cotton was pleased to join them. In his "Notes on Buzz a Buzz" which he wrote some years later (see Chapter Eight) he made the following remarks about his stay:

"I had pitched my little tent in a grass meadow, close to Lord Napier's snug house. His hospitality by day was unbounded, but straitened as he was for room by night, he was not sorry to entertain a guest who delighted in camping out, and brought with him the means of doing so."
It is clear from this expedition that Cotton had regained some of his old skill as a versatile traveller and could adapt himself to the outdoor life when necessary.

Almost certainly he returned to England in the early autumn, as he is recorded in the Clergy Lists for 1855 as a preacher at Woodford Bridge. As Woodford Bridge was only a few miles from the family home in Leytonstone, his father had probably arranged for him to assist in services there, as a first step towards him gaining a curacy.

In December 1855 he was appointed to his first curacy since his return from New Zealand at St Mary Redcliffe in Bristol. A small insight into his state of health during this period can be gained from one of Phoebe's letters. Writing to her friend, Eliza Hobhouse, in April 1856 she stated: "He (WCC) was with us last Sunday and though poorly in the morning, walked through the wet to church and, without any pressing, preached a very characteristic sermon."[5] He resigned his curacy at Bristol towards the end of May 1857. Earlier in that month his peace of mind received another blow when he heard of the death of his favourite sister, Phoebe, at the age of 39. She had fallen ill and was found to be suffering from pulmonary tuberculosis. In the spring of 1857 she travelled to Torquay for the warmth and pure air. But after a few weeks her condition worsened and she died there on 7th of May. She and her sister, Sarah, had been the ones with whom Cotton had corresponded most frequently during his stay in New Zealand and, undoubtedly, her death saddened him deeply. Perhaps it was partly to recover from this tragic event that in the summer he set off on another Continental tour, during which he visited Avignon and Paris.

William Charles Cotton MA
1813 - 1879
Priest, Missionary and Bee Master

The church of St Mary Redcliffe, Bristol.
(Photograph courtesy of Judges of Hastings www.judges.co.uk).

Sarah Acland

Sarah, a clever and gifted child, grew up to be a considerable scholar – a noteworthy achievement for a young lady in her day. William Charles, her eldest brother, had taught her Latin and Greek and she subsequently learnt French, German and Italian, as well as having some knowledge of Spanish, Dutch and Norwegian. Once, whilst staying in a guesthouse in Norway, some local people mistook her for the landlady of the house - much to her considerable amusement. In the summer of 1846 she married Henry Acland.

William Charles Cotton MA
1813 - 1879
Priest, Missionary and Bee Master

A portrait of Sarah Acland after George Richmond RA 1846.

During their undergraduate days in Oxford, William Charles had been a close friend of Henry Acland. On visits to Walwood House, Acland had met Sarah. Gradually their friendship blossomed until Henry decided to ask the father for permission to marry her. At first William Cotton refused but when, in 1845, Henry gained the vacant Lee's Readership in Anatomy at Christ Church, her father gave his sanction to the marriage. In July 1846, shortly after their wedding, Sarah left Leytonstone to live with her husband in Oxford. In due course they had eight children - seven sons and one daughter.

One member of the family wrote this description of her as the children were growing up: "It is very difficult to think of the family life in

Broad Street (their home in Oxford) without one figure rising above all others - that of the devoted wife and mother around whom everything centred. She was a most remarkable woman in every way."[6]

It is said that, for someone of such a devout and formal background, she had a great sense of fun and good humour. In addition to her linguistic talents, she had become an accomplished pianist and had a fine contralto voice. Her husband went on to become the Regius Professor of Medicine at Oxford in 1857 and President of the Medical Council in 1874.

A Friend and Contemporary

During this period when little is known of Cotton's movements, let alone his thoughts and opinions, it is interesting to note what his contemporaries at Oxford wrote about him. One such gentleman was Charles Lutwidge Dodgson, better known as Lewis Carroll, the author of numerous stories and poems, including "Alice in Wonderland" and "Through the Looking Glass." Charles Dodgson graduated at Christ Church in 1846, took his MA in 1849 and became a Lecturer in Mathematics at the College in 1852.

Although at this time WCC only used his College rooms occasionally, it is likely that the two were acquaintances. However the only evidence for this is contained in Charles Dodgson's diaries. He first met Cotton on 9th June 1857. His diary states: "I breakfasted with Marshall to meet Cotton, (brother of my friend[7]), a senior student, seventh on the list. He photographs on paper, and is going to present the Common Room with his pictures. He wanted me to join in a photographic tour of France, where he means to live out in the fields in a tent. I do not much fancy the plan."

It is apparent from these remarks that WCC not only had a keen interest in photography but also that he had become a skilled practitioner. In addition he had sufficient enthusiasm for this pursuit to propose a visit to France and, despite his mental troubles, he was well enough to contemplate a tent expedition. According to Dodgson's diary the pair met again on 1st July 1857 at Old Hummus, an hotel near Covent Garden. Unfortunately nothing is known of what transpired at this meeting nor of any subsequent contact between them.

Charles Lutwidge Dodgson at the age of 24 - a photograph probably taken by Reginald Southey.

NOTES AND REFERENCES - CHAPTER SIX

[1] Ruth Etherington "Reverend William Charles Cotton" Auckland-Waikato Historical Societies Journal August 1980.

[2] Sarah Selwyn's letter to Reverend Edward Coleridge 3rd November 1848.

[3] Letter from his father dated 1st March 1853 Ms Acland BL.

[4] Chapter Book, Christ Church, Oxford - D&C i.b.10,f.156v.

[5] Ruth Etherington "Reverend William Charles Cotton" Auckland-Waikato Historical Societies Journal April 1980.

[6] J B Atlay "Sir Henry Wentworth Acland" page 378.

[7] A reference to Cotton's brother, Henry, who was a judge on the standing Counsel for the University of Oxford(see Appendix VIII).

William Charles Cotton MA
1813 - 1879
Priest, Missionary and Bee Master

CHAPTER SEVEN

VICAR OF FRODSHAM - 1857 to 1879

Difficult Times

In the summer of 1857, on the resignation of Reverend J R Hall, the Dean and Chapter of Christ Church, Oxford, appointed Reverend Cotton to the living of Frodsham in Cheshire. On 5th August he travelled, accompanied by his dogs, from the family home in Leytonstone to his new incumbency. However the journey did not pass without incident. Whilst travelling on the Oxford, Worcester and Wolverhampton Railway he refused to leave his dogs in the guard's van and, despite instructions to the contrary, insisted on taking them into the carriage.

A few days later he was charged by the Railway Company with obstructing their officers in the discharge of their duty. Further it was alleged that he attempted to get into a carriage whilst the train was in motion. The magistrates at Dudley found the charges proved and he was fined 10 shillings on each count. Maybe this episode amounted to nothing more than an unfortunate misunderstanding, or perhaps it shows that Cotton felt it to be beneath his dignity to quietly accept instructions from mere railway officials.

In addition to the worry caused by this incident, he brought with him a number of personal troubles with which he had been struggling for some time. The sad loss of his sister, Phoebe, just a few months before, had not helped matters. One can imagine Cotton, in these first few weeks and months, living in the old, and rather squalid, seventeenth century vicarage, cut off from his family and friends in Leytonstone, feeling lonely and despondent. Probably these feelings were intensified when he realized the magnitude of the job that lay before him.

William Charles Cotton MA
1813 - 1879
Priest, Missionary and Bee Master

For instance, the dismal state of the church, with its huge, ugly galleries, and antiquated box pews, not to mention the cracked and bulging walls of the south aisle. As he spoke with his Churchwardens he would soon realize the enormous size of the parish and the task he faced if he was to prevent the further spread of nonconformity.

Soon there were many criticisms circulating in the town about his apathy and his unwillingness to tackle the problems facing the parish. One of his fiercest critics was the previous incumbent, the Reverend John Robert Hall. On 27th March 1857, in a letter to Christ Church, Hall had announced his intention to resign the living in "about three months time" and then went on to express his grave concern about the state of affairs in the townships. He described the situation as follows: "The Parish of Frodsham is very extensive, being over 32 miles in circumference, with a Population of 6400 and containing 8 townships, each with its own Poor Rates, Highway Rates and Parochial Officers."[1] (For more about the town at this time see Appendix VII). He explained that until 1844 only the town and lordship of Frodsham had a church and resident minister, and consequently the number of Dissenters had increased rapidly in the surrounding districts. When he first came to Frodsham he found "no less than ten meeting houses[2] in the Parish." Since that time the ancient chapel at Alvanley had been rebuilt and new churches at Norley (1844) and Kingsley (1850) had been erected. During his incumbency he had raised £6000 for new churches and schools, but he argued the effects had been largely neutralized by the lack of endowments.

So Reverend Hall was suggesting that, before the Dean and Chapter appointed a new vicar, better provision should be made for the outlying townships. He proposed that the vicarial tithes of five of the townships should be taken from the Frodsham vicar and granted to the clergy of those districts. In compensation the Dean and Chapter should grant £150 of rectorial tithes to the new incumbent at Frodsham. Hall concluded that this would mean some loss of revenue to the new vicar but it would help to remove the growing dissatisfaction felt in the townships.

Despite Hall's pleas for immediate reform, the Dean and Chapter proceeded to appoint Reverend Cotton to the living, without making any changes. It is an interesting fact that Cotton came to Frodsham with a fine testimonial from the Reverend George Madan, Vicar of St Mary Redcliffe and from two other priests from neighbouring Bristol churches. George Madan had known him for one year and nine months and recommended him to the Bishop of Chester with every confidence. Rather unusually WCC's induction did not take place until 6th November when Reverend Edward Wolfenden of Alvanley presided.

The ancient parish of Frodsham with its eight townships.
(From a map issued in conjunction with the booklet "The Ancient Parishes, Townships and Chapelries of Cheshire by FI Dunn 1987.
This extract is shown here by kind permission of the
Cheshire and Chester Archives and Local Studies Service).

It was not until the autumn of the following year that the Dean and Chapter requested Reverend Hall to give them more details on the state of affairs in the parish. In his reply Hall explained how the endowments in Norley, Kingsley and Alvanley were extremely small and reiterated his plan that the Frodsham Vicar should transfer the vicarial tithes to these townships. In return he should be compensated by Christ Church from the rectorial tithes. He drove home his argument as follows: "There is of course a strong anti-Church feeling, especially in the distant townships, which calls for skilful management and untiring energy on the part of the Vicar and Clergy; and I think nothing would do so much to disarm hostility and to strengthen the hands of the Clergy and the good Churchmen in the Parish, as giving up the Tithes of the several Townships to the respective Incumbents."[3] He pointed out that under his plan Vicar Cotton would suffer some loss but this could be considered preferable to allowing the present unsatisfactory situation to continue.

Hall concluded his letter thus: "I hear the most sad accounts from Frodsham of poor Cotton. He seems to have fallen into a state of torpor and listless apathy, and takes no interest in anything. I propose going to Frodsham next week for a few days in the hope of stirring him up." Reverend Hall was not Cotton's only critic. Many others were deploring his despondency. The Bishop of Chester called him a "lunatic priest" and complained that he was failing to pay the curates' stipends.

One wonders what were the reasons for this apathetic behaviour on Cotton's part. Was it that he had been obliged to take the living at Frodsham once more to please his father? Or was he so unwell that he could not cope, especially with the problems of such a large parish? He must have resented Hall's constant interference and perhaps felt strongly that he should not be expected to submit to a plan for endowments which involved him in a loss of revenue.

According to the Reverend Tyas, vicar of Kingsley, in a memorial to the Dean and Chapter dated July 1861, Cotton approved of the Reverend Hall's plan for the augmentation of the township livings, but had prevaricated about making any formal arrangements. Reverend Edward Wolfenden, minister of Alvanley Church, writing to the Dean

of Christ Church in June 1862, confirmed this state of affairs. He went on to regret that "such a parish as Frodsham should be so situated in church matters as it is at present. It is unnecessary to go into particulars. I dare say you are aware of the nature of the case, things may all be summed up in one word "deplorable."
Reverend Wolfenden added in a footnote to his letter: "Mr Cotton looks well and to all appearances seems to be in perfect health. No doubt his mind is more or less diseased."[4]

Clearly Cotton, struggling with his own depressed state of mind, was finding it difficult to cope with the question of endowments, along with all the work involved in conducting day to day church business.

In August 1862 Reverend Hall wrote to Archdeacon Clerke with yet another proposal. He argued that the location of Frodsham church was a great handicap and a chapel of ease was urgently needed in the middle of the town: "In wet or stormy weather it is impossible for females or aged people to climb the hill to Church and they are tempted to go to Dissenting Chapels." "But," according to the Reverend Hall, "poor Cotton is incapable of doing anything......... everything must be done for him and yet he is very sensitive and jealous of the interference of others."[5] Reverend Hall even offered to take over the parish and run it on Cotton's behalf, but not surprisingly, the new vicar refused.

Hall seems to have been a zealous and reforming priest who, even after he had left Frodsham, was full of ideas for the betterment of the parish. Evidently he had no time for an incumbent who was beset by personal problems and who found it difficult to cope with his new situation. In a letter dated November 1862 he wrote: "I hear that Cotton sits in a chair all day and never leaves the house except when he is summoned to a funeral or something of the kind." He went on to say that Cotton had no curate and the sick were not visited; he scrambled through two services on Sundays and had given up the third. He continued: "I am told the Church is almost deserted and that the Church people are extremely dissatisfied. Meantime dissent, which had been losing ground in the Parish, had come in like a flood and threatens to sweep all before it."[6]

Bats and Owls in the Chancel

Another serious problem facing WCC at this time was the condition of the church, an ancient structure of mainly Norman and Late Perpendicular architecture. However it was the later additions, which were the main cause for concern. In November 1865, along with other criticisms, the Bishop of Chester complained that he had found the chancel to be in "a discreditable state." A newspaper report in the early 1870s even spoke of bats and owls in the chancel.

The old box pews and galleries of the Church in the 1870s, with the white washed walls much in evidence.
Photograph by kind permission of the Governing Body of Christ Church, Oxford.

William Charles Cotton MA
1813 - 1879
Priest, Missionary and Bee Master

Reverend Cotton, third from the right, sitting at the grave of the curate, Reverend Robert Williams who died in January 1871.
To the right is the Wright family vault. The man wearing the cap standing between the gravestones is Samuel Aston, the sexton. In the background is the Frodsham Parish Church as it was prior to the restoration of 1880-82.
Photograph by kind permission of the Governing Body of Christ Church, Oxford.

According to a report sent to Christ Church in 1868, the church had a very debased south aisle and three gloomy galleries on the north, south and west sides. The pews were high backed and narrow, with high doors. The south aisle, which had been constructed in the early eighteenth century, had a number of defects, including bulging and cracked walls, and the huge ugly galleries made the interior dark and sombre. These, and other problems with the fabric of the church, must have fallen onto Cotton's shoulders like a crushing weight, and it was some years before he felt able to tackle them.

The Long Wrangle over Endowments

In the summer of 1863, according to a letter from the Reverend Tyas, the vicar of Kingsley, the plan for augmenting the township livings was still under discussion between the various parties. The obstacle to an agreement seemed to be the townships of Helsby and Manley where there was no church and therefore no one to receive the tithes except Vicar Cotton. The Bishop of Chester suggested these townships should be left out of any agreement. Reverend Tyas, with due deference, thought this to be a good plan. He wrote: "It is likely that if a Deed to that effect were presented to Mr Cotton he would execute it."[7] Tyas was on good terms with Cotton and requested that his name was not mentioned in any future discussions on this matter. Cotton was already vexed with him for his previous interference.

Probably it was the stress caused by his difficulties in coping with Church matters and the wrangle over endowments that brought on another bout of mental illness. But the final straw may have been the news that his father had decided that the Walwood estate should pass, not to him as the eldest son, but to his mother, and then, on her death, to his brother, Henry. This must have been a severe blow to his self-esteem.

In the autumn of 1865 his condition deteriorated and arrangements were made for him to visit Dr Tuke's asylum in Chiswick. This small private mental hospital had been run for over a hundred years by a family of doctors who were noted for their humane ideas on how to treat the mentally sick. From 1837 to 1892 its premises were Manor Farm House, Chiswick Lane. At the time Cotton stayed there in 1865, Dr Seymour Tuke had taken charge. He served as a governor of St George's Hospital, Chiswick, and was a member of many medical societies. Besides being a well-qualified and experienced doctor, he had a reputation for courteous and kindly ways.

William Charles Cotton MA
1813 - 1879
Priest, Missionary and Bee Master

Dr Tuke's asylum at the Manor Farm House, Chiswick, in the mid nineteenth century - sometimes referred to simply as the Manor House.

Before he left for his visit to Chiswick, Cotton had started to pay the tithes to the incumbents of Alvanley and Kingsley, but now that he was absent from the parish neither of these gentlemen were receiving their endowments. However by November 1865 the Vicar had consented to continue the payments and the sums owing were also paid. At the same time the Bishop was still trying to arrange a formal agreement between WCC and the Dean and Chapter of Christ Church.

It would appear that this agreement was still not completed for a number of years because, in June 1868, Cotton was himself urging the implementation of the scheme.

The Death of William Cotton

Another distressing event for the Frodsham Vicar occurred in December 1866 with the death of his father. Although he had many demands placed on him by his father, William Charles had a deep love and respect for him. Almost certainly William Cotton had been ill for some months, but even so WCC was deeply saddened by his death. Nevertheless when the terms of the will were discussed, he probably felt once more a deep sense of hurt at the way he had been passed over in favour of his brother, Henry.

Slow Progress

In the late 1860s, after his treatment at Dr Tuke's asylum, Cotton's mental illness seems to have subsided and he made some progress with the various problems that he faced in the parish. Early in 1870 he arranged for the architects H Woodyear of Guildford and Messrs Hay of Liverpool to draw up plans for the restoration of the church. He received their proposals towards the end of the year. However in the meantime, by a resolution of the Easter Vestry, an architect from Manchester had been asked to draw up a report on the stability of an arch in the Chancel. A few months later Cotton became concerned to find that this architect had gone beyond his remit and drawn up a report for the restoration of the whole church. In a letter to Christ Church he wrote rather scathingly of him. He called him a gentleman of "no great celebrity." He was clearly anxious that restoration work should only be carried out under the direction of a first-rate architect. He made it clear that he would only allow his monies, that is, sums contributed by his family and friends, to be used if this condition was met. Similarly he hoped that Christ Church would adhere to the same principle when they were considering the release of any funds for the Frodsham Church.

In 1871 the plan to build a temporary Iron Church in the middle of the town came under active consideration. As mentioned earlier the idea of providing a chapel of ease had been first proposed by the Reverend J R Hall in 1862. At the same time the Anglicans were well aware of the growing threat posed by the Dissenters, especially the Methodists. Mr Thomas Hazlehurst of Runcorn had already donated a large sum for the construction of the Eden Chapel at Five Crosses, Overton, which lay within a quarter of a mile of the Parish Church. In the early 1870s, with financial help from Mr Hazlehurst, the Methodists were proposing to build another new church near the centre of Frodsham - the future Trinity Chapel.

With these developments Cotton became convinced of the need for the construction of a chapel of ease. Writing to Christ Church in 1872, he gave his reasons for choosing a temporary Iron Church, which could be erected quickly. Firstly, although his plans were not yet ready, he felt there was a great need to have alternative accommodation in place for when restoration work started and the parish church had to be closed. Secondly, he knew that a church in the town was urgently required to counter the threat posed by the Methodists. He substantiated his argument with the following statement:
"An inhabitant of Runcorn, Mr Hazlehurst, has a large sum of money under his control, which he employs in putting up gorgeous Wesleyan Chapels often in places where they are not required. The existing chapels in Frodsham are not half, or even a quarter filled, and yet he has begun a new one on which he is going to spend six or seven thousand pounds! He has some years ago built one within a quarter of a mile of the Vicarage and two enormous buildings in Runcorn."[8]

For some time Sunday evening services had been held in the Girls' School in Church Street, Frodsham, but the Vicar felt this arrangement was unsatisfactory. The schoolroom would only seat about ninety people and he complained it could not be kept as clean and tidy as a place of worship should be. There had been some opposition from amongst the gentry to the building of a church in the town but they now agreed with the plan. Cotton argued that the outlay on an iron church would not be excessive. The total cost would be only £600 - 00, with an additional £200 - 00 for heating, lighting and furniture. The Marquis of Cholmondeley had agreed to provide the land and the building could be erected in about four weeks and would soon be in working order.
Having gained the consent of Christ Church and the Bishop of

Chester, Cotton acted remarkably quickly. By the end of the month he was informing the College authorities that the Iron Church was now under construction and was asking them for a contribution of £100-00 towards the cost of "lighting, warming and fencing."

Restoration Plans

With the Iron Church nearing completion, the Vicar turned his attention once more to the renovation of the Parish Church. In a letter to Reverend Faussett, Treasurer of Christ Church, dated March 1872, he set out his plans for raising £6000 for the restoration. Perhaps, understandably, he referred to the project as this "arduous undertaking" and expressed his appreciation of the "kindly and co-operative spirit" with which his proposals had been greeted in Oxford. Later in the letter he mentioned that those who once opposed his plans were now eager to see improvements take place. He wrote: "I am reaping the fruit of having bided my hour."[9]

He went on to speak of the success of Helsby Church, which had been opened in 1870. There was a small but steady congregation of 70 to 80 people in the morning and as many as 250 in the afternoon, whereas before there had been as few as 5 or 10 attending the services held in the schoolroom. The content and phrasing of these letters suggest that Cotton was handling these matters well and, when he was not suffering any ill health, he was in complete control of the situation.

The building of the Iron Church was completed by Easter Week 1872, which shows just how much he could accomplish in his more stable periods. Further it is interesting to note that this new church was paid for entirely by the parish, except for a few donations by Cotton's relatives and a contribution of £100 - 00 from Christ Church. In June 1872 he sent a copy of Woodyear's survey of the Parish Church to Oxford, asking the College for their contribution towards the cost of the restoration.

William Charles Cotton MA
1813 - 1879
Priest, Missionary and Bee Master

St Paul's Church, Helsby, constructed between 1868 and 1870 under the direction of the architect, John Douglas, of Chester. Note its distinctive roof and steeple.

The Iron Church as it appeared in 1985 before it was moved nearer to Ashley House and before the frontage was modernized.

William Charles Cotton MA
1813 - 1879
Priest, Missionary and Bee Master

The Vicarage House

Yet another project with which Cotton busied himself at this time was the renovation of the Vicarage House. The building originally consisted of a small cottage, probably dating from the early seventeenth century, to which additions had been made from time to time. The house itself contained a moderate sized dining room, a drawing room, a kitchen, a small pantry, a small back kitchen and a cellar. On the first floor there were four bedrooms, with two "very poor" attics. Writing to Christ Church in January 1872 he stated that when the living was offered to him in 1857 the condition of the vicarage was described as "not good." He added, "a much stronger epithet might have been used." He received £108 - 00 for dilapidations from the former vicar and, during the last few years, had spent several times that amount in carrying out essential repairs. Since the day he moved in, he had found that the house had some major faults. The floorboards in most of the upper rooms were in such a state that he said it was like walking on thin ice. The house badly needed a study, preferably adjacent to the front door, to which he could invite his parishioners when they called to see him.

A painting of the Frodsham Vicarage circa 1830. On the left of the house are the Parish Church, the schoolmaster's house and the Frodsham Grammar School. Reproduced here by kind permission of Mr Simon Crooks.

William Charles Cotton MA
1813 - 1879
Priest, Missionary and Bee Master

In June 1868, in another report to Christ Church,[10] Cotton stated that "the kitchen is very old but in good repair", but when asked does the Vicarage suffer from damp, or any other inconveniences, he gave this terse reply: "Wind, Water, Rain and Rats" - which would seem to sum up admirably the poor condition of the property. In another letter he explained that the bricks in this part of the country were of a very porous nature so that heavy, driving rain caused many of the exposed walls to be damp. He suggested applying tiling to the walls of the upper storey to prevent this happening. The Inspector of Livings, Mr W Paver, who visited the House in October 1871, concluded: "the whole House is in want of thorough repair, principally in consequence of being badly built."

In the autumn of 1872 Cotton engaged John Douglas, a well-known Chester architect, to draw up plans for the enlargement and renovation of the vicarage. A few weeks later, he sent copies of these plans to Christ Church, including a builder's estimate that the cost of the entire works would be £976-10-5. It is interesting to compare this figure with the £600 which was the estimated cost of building the Iron Church. The College then asked for an independent report. In response, Mr J W Hugall, surveyor, found the Vicarage House to be in a very dilapidated state owing, he said, not to want of preservation but due to faulty construction. In his letter he approved of the plans drawn up by Mr Douglas for the enlargement of the house, the strengthening of its weak points and the provision of the additional accommodation that was required. In their turn Christ Church agreed to the scheme and confirmed that Cotton should apply to the Queen Anne's Bounty Board for the necessary funds to carry out the project. The Board administered a fund created by Queen Anne in 1704 to receive the first-fruits[11] and tenths confiscated by Henry VIII. She had directed that the money should be used, inter alia, for capital grants to poorly endowed benefices. From 1803 the fund was empowered to make disbursements for the building and repair of parsonage houses. Between 1809 and 1820 it received grants of over £1 million from Parliament and at times large private benefactions. In due course the application to this fund was approved and the Vicar gave instructions for the work to be undertaken.

William Charles Cotton MA
1813 - 1879
Priest, Missionary and Bee Master

The scheme involved a huge reconstruction of the front and the west side of the house. The roof was to be completely rebuilt with a number of new gables, a tower erected at the front and the drawing room extended to include a large bay window. Knowing that such a large scale rebuilding would take a long time, Cotton decided to have another residence built to provide him with a comfortable place to live for the duration of the work. Probably after his father's death in 1866, he inherited sufficient money to make this expenditure possible. Once again employing John Douglas as his architect, he had a house constructed on land at the junction of Red Lane and Fluin Lane, Frodsham. He decided that it should bear the name Stapleton House. On completion of the work on the vicarage he sold this mansion to Edward Abbott Wright of Castle Park who wanted to provide a home for his daughter, Julia, and her husband, George Garratt.

The sandstone plaque on the tower of the Old Vicarage with a Latin inscription telling of the enlargement and renovation of the house during Cotton's incumbency.

William Charles Cotton MA
1813 - 1879
Priest, Missionary and Bee Master

The inscription, as far as it can be made out, reads as follows:

"DECANO ADMORUM REVERENDIS ALUMNIS OVE AEDIS CHRISTI

ADVENTII BENEFICENTIA V ANNAE REGINAE (B.M.)

NECNON PROPRIO SUMPTU HANC DOMUM VETUSTATE FOEDAM ET PROPE DILAPSAM

REFECIT AMPLIFICAVIT DECORAVIT

W C COTTON M A VICARIUS EIUSDEM AEDIS OLIM ALUMNUS

MDCCCLXXIII."

"Through the Dean and the reverend members of Christ Church, the beneficence of Queen Anne, and with his own money, W C Cotton, MA, vicar and alumnus of the same House, has decorated, rebuilt and extended this house which was dirty and nearly derelict. 1873."

A photograph of Reverend Cotton taken in his early sixties

William Charles Cotton MA
1813 - 1879
Priest, Missionary and Bee Master

The new vicarage must have been a great improvement on the old house. It had a large, elegant drawing room and a very fine dining room, the walls of which were covered in handsome oak panelling. At the rear of the house stood the library with Cotton's huge collection of books. Below was the cellar in which the Vicar stored his wine. The latter had four rooms, two of stone and two of brick, possibly built at different times. On the outside wall above the former doorway is the inscription "In vino veritas. Real good wine. Good wine needs no bush" - the latter phrase being an old saying dating from the time when English taverns often had the sign of an ivy bush over the door to indicate the excellence of the liquors served within.

A side view of the tower. To the left is the main door, at the foot of which is the Maori inscription "Haere Maie Te Manuwiri" ("Welcome to the Stranger from Afar").

William Charles Cotton MA
1813 - 1879
Priest, Missionary and Bee Master

*Stapleton House with its typical
John Douglas style of architecture.
Sadly this fine Victorian mansion was demolished in the 1950s.*

*Stained glass windows in the vestibule of the former vicarage,
showing the arms of Christ Church, Oxford, on the left,
and those of the Bishop of Chester on the right.*

The west side elevation of the house as it appears today.
The older part of the building can be clearly seen to the rear.

The Other Side of the Coin

At the same time that he was busy with these projects, Cotton was still subject to periods of manic depression. He had suffered from this disability for many years but it seems to have grown worse as he grew older. This mental instability, aggravated by misfortune and stress, led gradually to more frequent spells of irrational behaviour.

This side of his character is reflected in a number of incidents that occurred in the early 1870s. In October 1872 a fracas took place at Pollard's Drapery Store in Frodsham involving Cotton and a Dr Spraltz. After some conversation between the two, the Vicar gave the gentleman a book. A little later he declared that he had only given the book provided that Dr Spraltz was willing to be examined on it. When the doctor refused, Cotton threw another book at him with such force that it cut open his head and broke "a pier glass."[12]

This incident was reported to Major Hitchin of Newton Hall (a Churchwarden) by a George Boydall. In the final paragraph of his letter Boydall asked if some restraint could be put on the Vicar as Dr Spraltz considered him to be dangerous.[13] A few days later there is more evidence that Cotton was passing through one of his bad spells. The Medical Officer, Frederick P Nears, wrote to say, "the Reverend W C Cotton's mind is very much off its balance. If he cannot be induced to restrain himself he will very speedily require to be placed under control."[14] He concluded that counsel from Dr Tuke might help Cotton to regain his equilibrium.

Later in the same month Henry Tiley, Cotton's manservant, received a complaint from a Mr Smith of Nicholas Street, Chester, that the Vicar should not be allowed to return to his (Smith's) house alone. "I must ask you to come with him, as my wife is much alarmed and insists on his not spending another night here, unless someone is in the house who is accustomed to him."[15] Tiley replied, rather unhelpfully, that he could do nothing about the matter.

In November 1872 W H Linaker, Solicitor and Assistant Clerk to Runcorn Union, wrote to the Reverend Canon John Barclay, Chairman of the Runcorn Board of Guardians, agreeing with his suggestion, that "if Mr Cotton's own relatives would not intervene to restrain him, then the Board should take some action."[16] Under the legal powers vested in them they had the authority to send any lunatic (pauper or otherwise) to the asylum under a certificate from a surgeon and a magistrate.

However this course of action seems to have been dropped in favour of seeking redress from the Bishop of Chester. In a letter dated 11th of January 1873 W H Linaker (Solicitor) acting on behalf of "certain gentlemen residing in the parish of Frodsham" stated that he wished to draw the attention of the Bishop to the conduct of Vicar Cotton and hoped that an enquiry would be made into his behaviour "in and out of the parish during the last three or four months."

Another incident took place later in the same month when Cotton was accused of refusing to pay a cab fare. The cabman applied to a magistrate in Chester for a summons against the Vicar. The cabman stated that he had requested payment without success and was told to take up the matter with the Churchwardens.[17]

Another complaint to the Bishop of Chester came from Mr G Hammond Danby, Principal of Overton Collegiate School, South Bank House, Frodsham. He stated that Cotton had called at his house at half past six on a Sunday morning and induced his Assistant Master to go with him to Northwich. The assistant, a 22 or 23 year-old Frenchman, was not well acquainted with the language or customs of this country. Mr Danby went on to say that the Vicar had detained the young man until nine o'clock on Monday morning, and that this sort of thing had happened several times. On sending a note to him, Cotton had come down to his house and "behaved himself in a most unbecoming and undignified manner." He is alleged to have said that the note was an insult and that Danby was forbidden to come into the Parish Church any more.

When the complainant engaged another Assistant Master the same thing happened again and he was obliged to dispense with his services. Furthermore Danby stated, "on Sunday evening last ....the Vicar accompanied by my late Assistant, met with one of our servants and made use of the most disgusting and filthy language such as cannot be repeated."

Finally, in his letter, Mr Danby asked whether the Church was to be scandalized by the Vicar's behaviour or would the Bishop take measures to put a stop to it. Unfortunately we do not know the outcome of these complaints and whether the Bishop took any action or not. However the various allegations made against Cotton indicate that he had indulged in some strange and, often spiteful, behaviour that, one can only suggest, resulted from his mental troubles. Another mitigating factor in considering his attitude in this incident was that he had had at least one other disagreement with Danby. A Mrs Warburton of Church Street, Frodsham, had complained on 14th August 1872 that Mr Danby was occupying her seat in the Church. Mr Danby had refused to move on the grounds that the Churchwardens had allocated the pew to him. Interestingly, the Vicar took the side of Mrs Warburton and stated that, as the seat was in the Chancel, it fell under his jurisdiction, and Danby had no right to be sitting there. On November 23rd 1872 Vicar Cotton wrote another letter in which he forbade Mr Danby "to intrude himself or any of your boys, or any one in your employ, in to the seat in the South Aisle where Mrs Warburton has sittings."[18]

Why Cotton was now referring to a seat in the South Aisle is not explained, but the whole episode suggests, firstly, that the Vicar did not see eye to eye with his Churchwardens and, secondly, that he seems to have had a long standing feud with Mr Danby.

Cotton's mental troubles can be probably attributed to a form of manic depression. One of the symptoms of this illness is an inability to manage money and he was always prone to spend extravagantly. In the past, when he had run short of money, it was his father who had helped him out, often, for instance, paying the stipends of his curates or paying bills incurred during his excursions on the Continent.

Further evidence of his tendency to overspend is shown by certain other events that occurred in 1872. In October of that year a Mr Lanes of the Manchester and Salford Bank wrote to Henry Linaker, the solicitor acting for the Churchwardens, stating that he had travelled on the train with Cotton to Warrington and managed to take possession of two cheque books. Mr Lanes urged Henry Linaker to secure the remaining cheque book before the Vicar had time to write for it.[19] Clearly the bank manager felt that he was not to be trusted to handle his money sensibly.

Two days later Mr Lanes informed Henry Linaker that he had received a letter from Cotton "of the wildest possible description." Lanes stated that he was complaining about bottles being robbed from his wine cellar. Also Cotton had drawn two drafts upon his brother and Dr Tuke, which Lanes had returned to him as "entirely irregular." He had advised him not to draw upon his friends - a course of action which would only offend them - but, he had explained, if necessary, to ask them for a remittance.[20]

In another letter, dated 28th October 1872, J R Pickmere, Treasurer for a Church Bazaar, stated he was returning a cheque for £6-00 signed by the Vicar to Henry Linaker. A Mrs Tuekett had received the cheque for goods supplied at a National School's Bazaar and the Bank would not honour it.

It is difficult to reconcile these spells of irrational behaviour shown in these incidents, with the way Cotton apparently dealt so ably with some of the problems facing the parish. He undertook the scheme to build the Iron Church, implemented plans for the reconstruction of the Vicarage and began to take steps towards the restoration of the Parish Church. One is forced to the conclusion that there were two sides to his character - the darker and the lighter side - and that it was in his more lucid times that he carried out these creditable schemes for the benefit of the Church and the local community.

NOTES AND REFERENCES - CHAPTER SEVEN

[1] Letter from Reverend J R Hall to Archdeacon Clerke dated 27th March 1857.

[2] By "meeting houses" no doubt he meant one or two Quaker meeting houses, but mostly Methodist chapels.

[3] Letter from Reverend J R Hall to Archdeacon Clerke, dated 1st November 1858, Boldon. Ms Estates 13 CC.

[4] Letter from Reverend E Wolfenden to Archdeacon Clerke 19th June 1862 Ms Estates 13 CC.

[5] Letter from Reverend J R Hall to Archdeacon Clerke 25th August 1862. Ms Estates 13 CC.

[6] Letter from Reverend J R Hall to Archdeacon Clerke, dated 24th November 1862, Boldon.

[7] Letter from Reverend Tyas to Archdeacon Clerke 6th August 1863.

[8] Letter to the Treasurer of Christ Church 24th January 1872.

[9] Ibid dated 7th March 1872.

[10] Reply to a circular sent out by the Senior Common Room to Christ Church livings dated June 1868.

[11] First-fruits or annates. The first year's revenue from an ecclesiastical benefice, formerly paid to the Papal curia.

[12] A large mirror, originally used to fill the space between windows.
[13] Letter from George Boydall to Major Hitchin 19th October 1872.

[14] Letter from F P Nears, Medical Officer, 21st October 1872.

[15] Letter from Mr Smith to Henry Tiley 31 October 1872.

[16] Letter from W H Linaker to Canon Barclay 2nd November 1872.

[17] Letter from W Sharp, Magistrates' Clerk, to W H Linaker 15th November 1872.

[18] Letter from Reverend Cotton to Mr Hammond Danby 23rd November 1872.

[19] Letter from W F Lanes (of the Salford and Manchester Bank) to Henry Linaker 24th October 1872.

[20] Ibid dated 26th October 1872.

CHAPTER EIGHT

THE GRAND BEE MASTER

Home Life, Church Schools and Final Days

Once he had settled down in Frodsham, Cotton continued to pursue his interest in beekeeping. For instance it is known that he worked with John Pollard, headmaster of the Endowed Boys' School at Overton, to improve the strain of bees and find those most suited to the New Zealand climate. It is said that Vicar Cotton wanted to see which hive of bees were the better navigators. One day he and John Pollard took two lots of bees over to Helsby, which is about three miles away. One lot was dyed with a yellow ochre and the other with blue ochre. At the appointed time they released them simultaneously and then hurried home to see which bees were the first to return to their hive. Unfortunately the result of the experiment is not recorded.

Further evidence that Cotton was fond of conducting experiments with his bees is contained in James F Robinson's book on bee-keeping practices.[1] He stated, "An apiary in which experiments are constantly being performed will never prove successful. The late Rev. W C Cotton at one time purchased fourteen good stocks in the same year, and lost all of them by experiments."

William Beamont, the Cheshire historian and contemporary of WCC, described in his history of Frodsham how he had seen Cotton at work with his bees. He explained how the Vicar, without any protection, had turned a hive of bees upside down and handled them at will. He

watched Cotton "select the queen from the rest, hold her up to the admiration of her subjects, and then restore her to them, without sustaining any hurt or sting.........."[2]
However there were times when he did suffer the occasional sting. One Sunday morning he was obliged to officiate in church with one eye partly closed from a bee sting. With his usual good humour he pointed out that at least "one unpleasant sight would be spared him, namely churchgoers asleep during his sermon.[3]

A fellow bee-keeper, William Carr of Newton Heath, near Manchester, met Cotton in August 1868 and kept up a correspondence with him to the last year of his life. He described the Frodsham Vicar as "a very kind, generous man and capital company." In his account of WCC in "The British Bee Journal," he tells how one day in June 1869 he pointed out to Cotton how the queen always turned her body downwards so that her head was below the horizontal line when laying an egg. After seeing this a few times WCC said he would correct the illustration in the next edition of "My Bee Book," as this was obviously true.[4]

The above mentioned bee enthusiast, James Robinson, who lived in Frodsham, paid this tribute to WCC's long campaign to make beekeeping more humane: "No apiarian has laboured more effectually for the abolition of the brimstone pit method of the late Rev W C Cotton."[5]

We have seen how over the years Cotton travelled extensively on the Continent for health reasons. Once, whilst waiting for a train on Cologne Station, he purchased from a bookstall a copy of "Schnurrdiburr" by Wilhelm Busch.[6] This book, profusely illustrated with clever and witty drawings, tells the comical story of a poor beekeeper, John Dull, and the amorous adventures of his daughter and mischievous nephew, with bees playing a prominent part in each escapade. These amusing tales appealed to Cotton's sense of humour and he decided to write his own version of the text.

William Charles Cotton MA
1813 - 1879
Priest, Missionary and Bee Master

The title page of Cotton's book "Buzz a Buzz," with the monogram of his initials.

The first page of the story showing the delightful style of drawings which appeared in the original book.

William Charles Cotton MA
1813 - 1879
Priest, Missionary and Bee Master

In September 1872 he published it under the title "Buzz a Buzz or The Bees - Done freely into English" but, in the manner of many Victorian authors, he did not give his name. However, on the title page, there is a monogram of his initials with the words "By the author of My Bee Book" around it. Furthermore the preface bears his initials WCC, dated Frodsham, Cheshire, September 1872. So the identity of the writer is quite clear. As Cotton stated in the preface, "the verses were written up to the pictures, rather than translated from the German text." He arranged for two versions to be printed - one in colour and the other in black and white. Phillipson & Golder published the Chester edition and Griffith & Farran the London one. Most critics agree that it is a clever and amusing work, probably one of Cotton's best pieces of writing.

Cotton relaxing in his library at the Vicarage. Artist unknown.

William Charles Cotton MA
1813 - 1879
Priest, Missionary and Bee Master

Another story related by William Beamont, was that "Papagay," Cotton's pet Portuguese parrot, often accompanied him on his foreign travels. On one occasion the pair were sightseeing on the field of Waterloo in Belgium when the Prince of Wales spotted them. Presented at his request, they are said to have sung "God Save the Queen" as a duet for him.[7]

According to the 1871 Census the Cotton household consisted of a boarder, the Reverend Richard Pilkington Watson, who was a curate at the Church. Henry Tiley, his manservant, who had come with WCC from Bristol. He was aged 28 and single. The cook, Mary Percival, aged 27 and unmarried. Finally there was Elizabeth Astle, the housemaid, aged 21. Shortly after this time Henry Tiley married Mary Percival and they had two children - a son, Arthur and a daughter, Eleanor. Tiley continued to work as Cotton's manservant, or "Major Domo," as he liked to call himself, right up to the time of Cotton's death. In later years he became an estate agent and one of H M Collectors of Taxes.

Beamont described how WCC loved to have pets at the Vicarage. Amongst these were a number of dogs and one of them, named Gip, became the pseudo author of numerous clever stories that appeared in the "The Field" and other journals. Each piece is a description of a tour that the dog and his master made together. These essays are quite remarkable for the natural thoughts and feelings about various things ascribed to Gip, the pretended author.[8]

Besides his pets the Vicar loved his extensive garden. Every year, when the roses were in full bloom, he held an "at home" when his parishioners were invited to enjoy the trees and the flowers and partake of an "al fresco" tea. One such occasion occurred in 1868 when he invited the children from the Frodsham Girls' School to come for tea at the Vicarage on the day before the summer holidays.

In later life Cotton was very active in discussions leading to the

William Charles Cotton MA
1813 - 1879
Priest, Missionary and Bee Master

formation of the British Beekeepers' Association and became one of its Vice Presidents. He also helped in the establishment of local, and then, national British Honey Shows. By the late 1860s he had gained a national reputation and in 1873 he judged at the Manchester Show. During his visit he saw and bought for ten pounds a magnificent glass super that weighed over 87lbs. "Super" is the old name for the upper part of the hive where the honeycombs are kept, the queen remaining in the lower part, laying her eggs whilst the brood is looked after by the worker bees. Clearly this was a very special super - the glass and the well-filled honeycombs together contributing to such a large weight. After the Manchester Show a lengthy debate ensued in bee-keeping circles as to whether such a super had been produced by natural means or whether it was the result of artificial feeding.

When he took this glass super to the first "Great Bee and Honey Show" at the Crystal Palace, Sydenham, near London, a year later, it was said to have attracted a great deal of attention - as no doubt did Vicar Cotton himself, as he made his way up to the judges' rostrum - a burly figure of over 20 stone dressed in trousers and "a quaint blouse."[9]

In his "Notes on Buzz a Buzz," written in September 1872, there is another reference to his weight. After a few remarks about Peggy, his first pony, he goes on to say "I have, alas, grown stout; and it requires a strong cob to carry twenty stone, and go lively under it as well."

Reverend Cotton had a huge library, including a collection of over two hundred British and European books on bees and apiculture that he bequeathed to the Parish of Frodsham. It is one of the finest collections of bee books of that period. Each book has a uniform leather binding with a queen bee logo and contains a bookplate showing the Cotton arms. The motto "Prodesse Quam Conspici" could well be translated as "Do good quietly" - a dictum which WCC almost certainly tried to follow in the less troubled periods of his life.

This large collection of books took up so much space in the Vicarage that in 1932 it was decided to deposit it with the Library of the Ministry of Agriculture, Food and Fisheries for their safekeeping. In 1987 the complete set of Cotton's bee books was transferred to Reading University Library. However the Parish of Frodsham still retains the ownership of the collection.

The queen bee logo and the bookplate showing the Cotton arms.

Schools

In the 1870s Cotton played a leading part in improving the provision of Church Schools in the parish. In those days there were two elementary schools in Frodsham - the Endowed School at Overton (formerly the Grammar School) for boys and, in the centre of the town, the National School for girls on Church Street. Until 1875 there was only one Infants' School which was situated to the rear of the Girls' School. In other parts of the parish church schools had been established at Norley, Kingsley, Alvanley and Helsby.

As in many other towns and villages by the 1860s, these schools were finding it difficult to cope with the increasing number of children. In 1870 the Liberal Government tried to find a remedy by passing the Education Act. One of its main clauses stated that where the voluntary bodies were failing to provide sufficient places then School Boards could be elected with powers to build new schools to fill the gaps. In November 1872 the trustees of the Church Schools were informed of a deficiency of 107 places for girls in Frodsham and of 60 places for infants at Overton. A number of public meetings were held and, after protracted debate, it was agreed to levy a 6d voluntary rate on landlords and tenant farmers to raise £600 for additional school accommodation. The meeting agreed that a Committee of Management should be established consisting of the existing trustees, plus four nominated persons from the Township and Lordship of Frodsham. Reverend Cotton and a Mr Edwards were empowered to draw up a circular explaining these changes and to have it delivered to all households.

Needless to say a great deal more work needed to be done to implement these decisions. In the next few years Cotton worked hard to see these improvements brought into being, along with similar changes in schools in some of the other townships. He wrote numerous letters and applications to the National Society seeking their assistance with funding. He even apologized for writing one letter in pencil, but he explained he had sprained a muscle in his back and had been forced to lie "supine" for three weeks. Plans to improve educational provision in the surrounding districts included an infants' school in Helsby and additional accommodation in Kingsley. By May 1874 a new Infants' School had been built in Helsby, which Cotton stated "I have built on my own responsibility, on condition that the tenant farmers who would have had to pay for a Board School, would guarantee a voluntary yearly subscription.........equivalent to a 3d rate."[10] This money, he wrote, together with the pupils' weekly pence and a government grant would provide a maintenance fund.

By June of the same year an extra schoolroom had been completed in Kingsley at a cost of £307 which meant that the boys and girls could be taught separately. The architect for this building, and probably for some of the other projects, was John Douglas of Chester - the same architect who had designed the new Vicarage House. However it was not until October 1876 that the work to enlarge the Girls' School and the Infants' School in Frodsham was finished at a total cost of £277. In the meantime a new Infants' School had been erected in 1875 at Five Crosses in Overton for which the Management Committee paid a total of £405.

In each of these projects Cotton had applied to the Church of England National Society for grants towards the cost of the building work and of the furniture and fittings. In each case the National Society responded sympathetically with a valuable contribution. It is worthy of note that Cotton was still working hard on these schemes until at least the end of 1876 and, except for the injury to his back, showed no sign of incapacity.

His Final Illness

For much of his life, especially during his time in Frodsham, Cotton suffered periodic bouts of mental instability. Once again it is hard to believe that the Vicar who, amongst other things, worked hard for the improvement of schools in the parish, could be the same man who, on some occasions, showed such bad temper towards certain parishioners. Towards the end of 1878 his health began to deteriorate again. Eventually he could no longer carry out his duties properly and, in 1879, a sequestration order was granted by the Bishop of Chester allowing John Ashton to take charge of the parish during the remainder of the Vicar's lifetime.

The relevant part of the order, dated 8th of April 1879, is as follows: "William, Lord Bishop of Chester to John Ashton of Frodsham in the County and Diocese of Chester, we are certified that William Charles

William Charles Cotton MA
1813 - 1879
Priest, Missionary and Bee Master

Cotton, Clerk, MA, Vicar of Frodsham, hath for some time past laboured under such an insanity of mind as to be rendered by it not only incapable of managing his own affairs and taking care of the rights of his vicarage but also of performing any part of his duty either in the said Church or Parish......... We do hereby decree all and singular the fruits, tithes, profits, oblations, dues and emoluments whatsoever belonging to the said vicarage to be sequestered for the uses of the aforesaid and do make you the said John Ashton sequestrator thereof................"[11]

John Ashton, as the sequestrator, was required to sign a bond obliging him to carry out his various duties in the parish on behalf of the Bishop. In the event of any failure to do so, he would be liable to forfeit the sum of £1000.[12]

In the early summer of 1879 arrangements were made for Cotton to return to Dr Tuke's asylum in Chiswick for more treatment. Sadly his condition grew worse and he died there on 22nd June 1879. According to the death certificate he had suffered from "ascites" for three weeks and "congestion of the brain" for one week before his death. He had grown exceedingly stout in the last ten years of his life, and so the accumulation of fluid in the abdomen (ascites) must have been extremely painful, not to mention the suffering caused by the crude means of expelling it.

The funeral service took place at St John the Baptist Church in Leytonstone, Essex, on Fiday 26th June and he was buried in the family grave in the churchyard. On the same day a commemorative service was held in the Parish Church at Frodsham. After prayers and hymns Reverend W T Giles of Chester gave the address. He spoke of how the strength of WCC's intellect had remained despite him being much weakened by the "terrible malady" from which he had suffered in his later years. He told of his unvarying kindness and how many people would miss him, especially the "aged poor." Reverend Giles concluded by remarking on how WCC had taken a great interest in the children of the parish - he loved to teach them and he loved to play with them. Out of respect for the memory of their late Vicar, shopkeepers closed their businesses up to the time of the service and most of the villagers drew their curtains.

William Charles Cotton MA
1813 - 1879
Priest, Missionary and Bee Master

The Cotton family vault in St John's Churchyard, Leytonstone, Essex.

The inscription on the gravestone giving the names of the members of the family who are buried here, including Cotton's mother and father, and two of his sisters, Phoebe and Agnes.

William Charles Cotton MA
1813 - 1879
Priest, Missionary and Bee Master

The memorial to Reverend William Charles Cotton in St Laurence Church. Unveiled in 1933 by the Vicar, Reverend Dr Myres, it was a gift of Mrs E J Milner of Fluin Lane, Frodsham.

In Conclusion

Reverend Cotton was a remarkable and accomplished man. He achieved a great deal during his lifetime, especially during his six years in New Zealand. When he returned to England in 1848 he faced many personal problems that led to a serious decline in his health. There is little doubt that he suffered from manic depression for which he seems to have had little or no medical treatment, except for his visits to Dr Tuke's asylum. Almost certainly his Continental excursions were a form of therapy that helped to occupy his mind and alleviate this mental condition.

Unfortunately he was still in this poor state of health when he arrived in Frodsham. Hence all the criticism of him - that he had "fallen into a state of torpor" and that "he sits in a chair all day and never leaves the house except when he is summoned to a funeral or something of the kind."

William Charles Cotton MA
1813 - 1879
Priest, Missionary and Bee Master

In the 1860s it is clear that his mental malady worsened. Several people made reference to his state of mind in letters to Christ Church and to the Bishop of Chester. Reverend Wolfenden of Alvanley writing to Oxford in 1862 said he wouldn't go into particulars about the parish but the present state of affairs was "deplorable," adding that, though Cotton looked well, his mind was "more or less diseased." Then in 1865 his condition deteriorated to such an extent that he had to visit Dr Tuke's asylum for several weeks.

However, after medical treatment, he seems to have made a sufficient recovery to be actively involved in various schemes for improvements in the Church and parish.

There is no doubt that Reverend Cotton was sometimes the cause of disagreements and bad feelings in the parish and that his apathy towards certain matters brought justifiable criticism upon him. However it is remarkable, bearing in mind how handicapped he was by ill health, that he did so much valuable work during his incumbency at Frodsham. It is a great tragedy that the life of such a clever and talented man, who could have achieved so much more than he did, was so frequently blighted by deep-seated mental problems. However, he will probably be best remembered for his work in New Zealand not only as a priest and missionary, but also for his contribution to the development of bee-keeping in that country, especially among the Maori. Similarly in England he made a lasting impact on bee-keeping practices and, despite his many problems, he left a legacy of various worthwhile improvements in the Parish of Frodsham.

However there is insufficient evidence to give any sort of final assessment of his standing with his fellow clergy, churchwardens and parishioners. Whether he was able to overcome his ill health in later years sufficiently to win general respect, it is difficult to say. The final verdict on his overall achievement must remain open and, to this extent, he continues to be an enigma.

NOTES AND REFERENCES - CHAPTER EIGHT

[1] James F Robinson "British Bee Farming: Its Profits and Pleasures" 1889.

[2] William Beamont "The Ancient Town of Frodsham" (1881) page 258.

[3] GE Mitchell "The Cheshire Beekeepers' Association – A Record 1899 – 1974." page 12.

[4] The British Bee Journal 1st January 1880.

[5] James F Robinson "British Bee Farming - Its Profits and Pleasures" 1889 page 104. The brimstone pit method was the traditional way of gaining access to the honey, as explained in Chapter I page 9.

[6] In the preface to "Buzz a Buzz" Cotton made an interesting reference to the Franco-Prussian War of 1870. He wrote: "The stall was covered with books about the late War. I had returned from a visit to the Battle Fields of 1870, and was sick of the subject. I wanted something of a more peaceful nature, and I was turning away, without making a purchase, when a book met my eye entitled "Schnurrdiburr."

[7] William Beamont "Frodsham - Some Account of Its History" 1881 page 257.

[8] Ibid page 257.

[9] Karl Showler "William Charles Cotton and the First Bees in New Zealand" in The British Bee Journal, June 1978.

[10] Letter to the National Society dated 16th May 1874.

[11] Copy of the deed of sequestration of the living at Frodsham to John Ashton dated 8th April 1879 Ms Estates 13 C C.

[12] Bond of Mr John Ashton for the performance of duty. EDP/1/5 CRO.

William Charles Cotton MA
1813 - 1879
Priest, Missionary and Bee Master

Glossary of Maori Words

ariki	chief, lord
atamira	bier, platform, stage
hahi, (haahi)	church, religion
hongi	smell, sniff; greeting by pressing noses
kai	a porridge made with flour and water; food, eat
kaihoro	glutton, gluttony, greedy, greed
kainga	dwelling place, home, village
karakia	prayer, chant, charm
kawakawa	pepper tree
koraha	open country
korero	a meeting
kawana	governor
mana	prestige, power
mihinare	missionary
minita	minister
moko	tattoo
pa	a fortified village

William Charles Cotton MA
1813 - 1879
Priest, Missionary and Bee Master

pakeha	a European settler
raupo(o)	reeds, rushes
ritenga Maori	Maori custom or practice
taiapa	fence, field
tamariki	children
tangi-hia	weep, grieve for
taonga	goods, property, wealth
tapu	holy, sacred
tohunga	priest, skilled person
utu	payment, revenge
Weteriana	Wesleyan
whare, ware	house, building
whare-karakia	church
wharepuni	meeting house

Appendix I
The Tomatin

According to Lloyd's Register for 1840, the *Tomatin was* a vessel of 428 tonnes. She was owned by Messrs Jamieson and registered in Glasgow. Captain Wingate had been appointed as her first master. For her maiden voyage she sailed to Port Adelaide, Australia, reaching there on 11th March 1840. On this voyage she had a crew of twenty-four.

Appendix II
The Flying Fish

As oe'r th'Atlantic wave was cast
   The first glad beams of day
Amazed I saw a fairy form
   Glance swift from out the spray

All silver were its glittering scales
   Its wings all black as night
Half fish half bird it seemed to mock
   The swallow in its flight
Now poised aloft its airy course
   It merrily pursues
Now plunging neath the wave its strength
   And loveliness renews

They say not sooth who tell that fear
   Impels it to this flight
So for is there - that upward bound
   Is leap of pure delight

Strange is it that a creature born
   Beneath the billowing sea
Should dare to soar above its home
   Tis passing strange - yet we

William Charles Cotton MA
1813 - 1879
Priest, Missionary and Bee Master

Poor sons of earth in this our life
  E'en stranger wonders find
Oh denizen of sea and air
  Which leave Thee far behind

The poet, tho' of woman born
  Led on by Fancy's fire
.... to the unseen world of song
  All undismayed aspire

Like the gay lark which aye doth soar
  And soaring aye doth sing
O'er earth o'er sea, thro' cloud thro' sky
  It floats with upturned wing

But lest his soul sh'd maddened be
  By draughts of that pure air
It falls again to Mother Earth
  Poor child of toil and care
Christian, a bolder flight is there!
  If Faith but give Thee wing
Thy soul well poised or then may reach
  The throne of Heaven's dread King

Tis not as yet a biding place
  For thy aspiring spirit
Our Father's house but now and then
  Like Sunday priests, we visit.

Journal Volume I pages 38 - 41.

William Charles Cotton MA
1813 - 1879
Priest, Missionary and Bee Master

Appendix III
Mary Anna Bumby

Mary Anna had come to New Zealand to act as housekeeper to her brother. It is said that she brought the bees because of his fondness for honey on his toast. She has been described as a beautiful lady with a complexion which entitled her to the name of "bonnie English rose." Her job as housekeeper at the mission came to a sad end when, in June 1840, he was drowned in a canoe accident in the Hauraki Gulf. She stayed on at Mangungu, and in December 1840, married Reverend Gideon Smales.

Mary Anna had been hostess to Governor Hobson and his party when they stayed at Mangungu in 1841 to get signatures from the local Maori chiefs for the Treaty of Waitangi. No doubt at some stage they talked about their bee-keeping experiences. It is rather surprising that during his stay with the Hobsons in May 1842, Cotton makes no reference to their common interest in bees. Even more remarkable is that he visited the Smales household in November 1842 and still made no mention of any bees there.

Appendix IV
The Treaty of Waitangi

Two years before Cotton set foot on the soil of New Zealand, the Treaty of Waitangi had been signed between Her Majesty's representative, the newly appointed Consul and Lieutenant Governor, William Hobson, and the chiefs of some of the tribes. The Treaty was signed at Government House, Waitangi, the home of the former Resident, James Busby, on 6th February 1840.

William Charles Cotton MA
1813 - 1879
Priest, Missionary and Bee Master

The main terms of the Treaty were firstly that the sovereignty of New Zealand should reside with Her Majesty, Queen Victoria, in return for the protection of the British Crown over all the people of New Zealand. Secondly the Government decreed that no land should be bought or sold in future without the sanction of the Crown.

Apppendix V

Lady Martin in her book "Our Maoris" had this to say about how the Maori clothed themselves during the time of her residence at Taurarua:

"The old picturesque dress, such as we have seen in Cook's Voyages, had given place to slop trousers and a blanket. A quainter spectacle one could hardly wish to see than a party of men squatting in a half circle, with their blankets drawn around their bodies, and hiding every part of their faces, except a bit of tatooed forehead and a pair of bright eyes. Then, whatever the habits of this people had been in their warmer ancestral home in the tropics, they eschewed much washing. Hands and blankets betokened that soap was a luxury. Their clothes had a combined scent of fish and tobacco and wood smoke. But we found them on acquaintance to be an independent, rough mannered, merry, kindly race, often obstinate and self willed, yet very shrewd and observant, and eager to learn English ways." (page 8)

Appendix VI
Governors Of New Zealand

Captain William Hobson R.N.   1840 - 1842

Lieutenant Willoughby Shortland R.N.   1842 - 1843
Acting Governor

Captain Robert Fitzroy R.N.   1844 - 1845

Sir George Grey   1845 - 1853

Captain William Hobson R.N.   1840 - 1842

Lieutenant Willoughby Shortland R.N.   1842 - 1843
Acting Governor

Captain Robert Fitzroy R.N.   1844 - 1845

Sir George Grey   1845 - 1853

Appendix VII
Frodsham in the Mid Nineteenth Century

When Cotton stepped down from the train on his arrival at Frodsham station in August 1857, what sort of place was he coming to?

In the late 1850s Frodsham was a small market town of just over 2800 inhabitants. Despite the upheaval caused by the building of the railway seven years before, it still retained its rural character, with its thatched cottages, well-stocked shops, quaint old inns and surrounded, as it was, by fields and countryside. Like most towns of its size, it had plenty of tradesmen, for example, blacksmiths, harness and saddle makers, wheelwrights, linen and woollen drapers. On the other hand the town had little industry, except for some quarrying on the hill, a salt works and an artificial manure manufactory on the River Weaver. For many years local administration had been divided between the township and the lordship. The majority of the people, numbering about 1860, lived in the township, many of them in the collection of houses, shops and inns clustered along the two principal highways, Main Street and Church Street.

On the other hand the lordship consisted mainly of the land that formerly belonged to the lord of the manor, that is the area of Overton, Bradley, Netherton and Woodhouses, plus a large part of Frodsham marshes. The ancient parish church stood foursquare in Overton, about half a mile from the centre of the town. Beyond the church stood Overton Hill, a lofty eminence, commanding splendid views over the River Mersey and the surrounding countryside. By 1857 a number of paths had been created on the hill and in the summer months many visitors came to enjoy these walks.

Many of the people were still engaged in farming, especially those living in the lordship and the surrounding countryside. Most kept dairy cattle or sheep, though there was some arable farming. In fact the district had become well known for the production of a fine crop of early potatoes every year.

By this time the town had a number of large and attractive residences, for example Crosbie House, Ashley House, The Gables, Park Place and The Manor House. During the next few years many more large houses were built as the railway enabled businessmen to travel greater distances to work. A contemporary reporter noted: "some of the houses have a modern appearance, but the cottages are mean-looking and in a dilapidated state."
The various inns – the Bear's Paw, the Queen's Head, the Commercial and the Golden Lion – were said to be reputable establishments and to be fitted up with every convenience for the comfort of visitors.

Appendix VIII
Sir Henry Cotton

Henry, the second son of William and Sarah Cotton of Leytonstone, Essex, had a distinguished career in the legal profession. In 1872 he was appointed standing counsel to the University of Oxford and five years later he became a lord justice of appeal. Shortly afterwards he received the honour of a knighthood and was sworn of the Privy Council.

Born at Leytonstone on the 20th of May 1821, he was educated at Eton College becoming a Newcastle Scholar in 1838. Whilst at Eton he showed a keen interest in sport, becoming "a wet bob" (an oarsman). He matriculated at Christ Church, Oxford, where he was a student from 1837 to 1852. He took his Bachelor's degree in January 1843, obtaining a second class in classics and a first class in mathematics.

He was called to the bar at Lincoln's Inn in January 1846. He soon acquired a large practice as a Chancery barrister and obtained his silk gown in December 1866. He was made a bencher of his inn in January 1867. After becoming a lord justice of appeal, in 1877 the University of Oxford conferred upon him the honorary degree of D.C.L. It is said of him that "as a judge, he was learned, painstaking and courteous, and he enjoyed the reputation of being one of the strongest members of the appeal court."[1]

In August 1852 he had married Clemence, the youngest daughter of the Reverend Thomas Streatfield of Chart's Edge in Kent. They had five sons and three daughters.

He died on 22nd February 1892 at his estate at Forest Mere, near Lipbrook in Hampshire, and was buried nearby in the churchyard of Milland.

[1] Oxford Dictionary of National Biography J S Cotton "Sir Henry Cotton" 1821 - 1892 rev. M C Curthoys.

William Charles Cotton MA
1813 - 1879
Priest, Missionary and Bee Master

BIBLIOGRAPHY

Marjorie Appleton "They came to New Zealand" Methuen 1958

J B Atlay "Sir Henry Wentworth Acland - A Memoir." Smith, Elder & Co, London 1903.

A G Bagnall & G C Petersen - "William Colenso" Wellington, Reed, New Zealand 1948

William Bambridge Diaries Alexander Turnbull Library, Wellington.

Peter Barrett "William Charles Cotton – Grand Bee Master of New Zealand 1842 – 1847" Published by the author 1997.

William Beamont "The Ancient Town of Frodsham" 1881

Sybil Birch "The Restoration of Frodsham Parish Church 1880-1882"

Isambard Brunel (Editor) "A Sketch of the Life and Character of Sarah Acland" Seeley and Co 1894

W C Cotton Journals No 1, 3 to 12. Dixson Library, State Library of New South Wales. Mf 110 Cheshire Record Office.

W C Cotton "My Bee Book" London 1842, Kingsmead Reprints 1970.

W C Cotton "A Manual for New Zealand Beekeepers" Facsimile reprint (1976) of the original edition printed in Wellington 1848.

W C Cotton "Buzz a Buzz or The Bees" 1872.

William Charles Cotton MA
1813 - 1879
Priest, Missionary and Bee Master

G H Curteis "Bishop Selwyn of New Zealand and of Lichfield: a sketch of his life and work." Kegan Paul, Trench & Co London 1889.

Charles Darwin "Voyage of the Beagle" J M Dent 1945

Allan K Davidson "Selwyn's Legacy. The College of St John the Evangelist Te Waimate and Auckland 1843 - 1992. A History." Published by the College of St John the Evangelist, Auckland 1993.

Reverend W Morris Davies "The Chronicle of Kingsley St John's Church School (1846 - 1996)."

Chris Dawson "Waitangi Treaty had links with First Beekeeper" New Zealand Beekeeper 1979.

Ernest Dieffenbach M.D. "Travels to New Zealand" John Murray, London 1843.

Ruth Etherington Journal of the Auckland-Waikato Historical Societies "Priest - Missionary - Beekeeper"(No 6 pp 1-6) 1980

John H Evans "The Churchman Militant: George Augustus Selwyn, Bishop of New Zealand and Lichfield" Allen & Unwin London 1964.

Helen M Hogan "Renata's Journey" Canterbury University Press 1994.

Ian Hopkins "Forty Two Years of Beekeeping in New Zealand 1874-1916, Some Reminiscences." 1916.

Edward Hubbard "The Work of John Douglas" The Victorian Society 1991.

Derek Hudson "An Illustrated Biography of Lewis Carroll" Constable London 1954.

William Charles Cotton MA
1813 - 1879
Priest, Missionary and Bee Master

Guy Lennard "Sir William Martin – The Life of the first Chief Justice of New Zealand" Whitcombe & Tombs.

Warren E Limbrick "The Poetical Missionary: the Reverend Thomas Whytehead 1815 – 1843."

Warren E Limbrick (Editor) "Bishop Selwyn in New Zealand 1841 - 1868" Dunmore Press, Palmerston North NZ 1983.

Mary Martin "Our Maoris" Society for the Promotion of Christian Knowledge, London 1884.

G E Mitchell "The Cheshire Beekeepers' Association - A Record 1899-1974"

Una Platts "This Lively Capital" 1971.

William Pember Reeves "The Long White Cloud" Viking 1987.

James F Robinson - "British Bee Farming: Its Profits and Pleasures" Chapman & Hall London 1889

H L Savell "Some Notes on the Cotton Family in Leyton" 1963 Leyton Public Libraries.

Sarah Harriet Selwyn "Reminiscences 1809-1867" Editor Enid A Evans. Typescript held by the Library of the Auckland War Memorial Museum 1961.

Karl Showler "William Charles Cotton and the first bees in New Zealand" British Bee Journal June 1978.

G Slater "Chronicle of Lives and Religion in Cheshire" 1891.

J M Stacpoole "A Guide to the Waimate Mission House" A R Shearer Government Printer, Wellington, New Zealand 1971.

M W Standish "The Waimate Mission Station" R E Owen, Government Printer, Wellington, New Zealand 1962.

William Yate "An Account of New Zealand" London 1843. Reprint Irish University Press 1970.

William Charles Cotton MA
1813 - 1879
Priest, Missionary and Bee Master

Index

A

Acland, Henry Wentworth 13, 30, 150, 166,167, 170, 221
    Sarah 150, 166,167, 221
Alvanley 172, 173, 174, 175, 179, 203, 209
Anglican Church 7, 14
Apiarian Society, Oxford 18
Arledge 163, 164
Arnold, Edward 64, 111
Ashton, John 205, 206, 211
Astle, Elizabeth 201
Aston 177
Atlay, J.B. 13, 30, 170, 221
Attorney General 59, 148, 156
Auckland 59, 60-61, 64, 66, 84, 115, 117, 120, 132-135, 137-138, 140, 143, 146, 148, 151-152, 156, 161-162, 170, 222- 223
Auckland Chronicle 123, 133
Australia 34, 51, 57, 214
Avignon 165

B

Bambridge, William 7, 34, 36, 38, 47, 55, 64, 101-104, 115, 122, 132, 135-136, 140, 147, 156-157, 161, 221
Bank of England 9, 15
Barclay, Rev. Canon John 191, 196
Bass Strait 51, 53
Baston 13
Battersea 34
Bay of Islands 7, 57, 58, 60, 63, 65, 73, 85, 88, 91-92, 120, 123, 134, 144
"Beagle" 73, 81, 122
Beamont, William 197, 201, 210, 221
Bees
    Captain Bough's 136, 152-153
    experiments 28, 197
    first honey bees in New Zealand 88-89, 216
    "Letters to Cottagers" 18, 21

William Charles Cotton MA
1813 - 1879
Priest, Missionary and Bee Master

"My Bee Book" 18, 19, 21, 27, 29, 30-31, 198, 200, 221
  transporting bees to New Zealand 27-29
Bible 19, 26, 39
Bishop's Auckland 134, 137-138, 140, 143, 152, 161-162
Bishop Broughton (Australia) 57, 109
Bishop of Chester 173-174, 176, 178, 182, 189, 191, 192, 205, 209
Bolland, William 112, 119, 120, 148, 149
  Mrs 149
Bough, Captain 136, 152-153
Boydall, George 191, 196
Bradley 219
"Bristolian" 59, 91, 158
British Bee Journal 198, 210, 211, 223
British Beekeepers' Association 202
British Honey Shows 202
Brown Alfred & Charlotte 125, 132
  Marsh 125
Brown Thomas 54
Buddle, Thomas 119
Bumby, John Hewgill 88, 89, 216
  Mary Anna 88, 89, 216
Busby 108, 151, 152, 217
Busch, Wilhelm 198
Butt George 102
  Henry 34, 99
"Buzz a Buzz" 164, 199, 200, 202, 210, 221

C

Cambridge 4, 24, 33, 34, 58, 59, 87, 100, 155
Campbell, Robert 57
Cape Brett 65
Cape Colony (S. Africa) 43
Cape Otway 53
Carpenter, Margaret 11
Carr, William 198
Carroll, Lewis 168-169
Chapel of Lambeth Palace 24
Chapman Mr 11

William Charles Cotton MA
1813 - 1879
Priest, Missionary and Bee Master

Chapman, Thomas 129
Chester 4, 183, 185, 191-192, 200, 206
Chigwell Grammar School 15
Chiswick 178, 179, 206
Cholmondeley Marquis 181
Christ Church, Oxford 4, 12, 13, 163-164, 167-168, 170-172, 174-177,
        179, 180-182, 184-185, 187, 189, 209-220
        Dean & Chapter 171-172, 174, 175, 179, 187
Church font (Waimate) 93
Church Missionary Society 24, 34, 57, 65, 74, 95, 134, 143
Church Schools 197, 203-204
Churton, Reverend 138, 158
Clarke, George 60, 68, 74, 76, 78, 104
Clerke, Robert 175, 195
Cole, Robert 34, 47, 84
Colenso Elizabeth 109-110, 132, 221
Colenso William 104, 108-110, 121, 132, 221
Coleridge, Reverend Edward 25, 32-33, 89, 132, 162, 170
Cologne Station 198
"Columbine" 93
Commercial Bay 136
Constantinople 164
"Cottage Gardener & Country Gentleman" 28
Cotton, William Charles
 -brothers and sisters 9-10
 -"My Bee Book" 18, 19, 21, 27, 29, 30-31, 198, 200, 221
 -seasickness 35
 -daily life on the Tomatin 39-40
 -climbing the rigging 42
 -a gift for Teddy 58
 -Sarah Selwyn's opinion 83-84, 110-111, 162-163
 -role at Waimate 86-87
 -living quarters 86-87
 -restoring garden 96
 -the new font 93
 -native dress 71, 73, 217
 -Maori children 101, 102-103
 -Collegiate School 102

William Charles Cotton MA
1813 - 1879
Priest, Missionary and Bee Master

-relations with father 106-107
-printing press 107
-friendship with Mrs Selwyn 110-112
-controversial remarks 123-124
-a game of chess 129
-Christmas Dinner 139
-Twelfth Night 140-141
-excessive spending 13-14, 20, 26, 142, 164, 193-194
-wood turning 145-146
-Taranaki 148-149
-marriage of sister, Sarah 150, 167
-his first bees in New Zealand 151-152
-letters 154
-farewell to New Zealand 155-156
-voyage home 157
-return to Enland 160
-illness 162-163
-travels on the Continent 163-165, 168
-preaching at Woodford Bridge 165
-curate at St Mary Redcliffe 165
-Vicar of Frodsham 171
-incident on railway journey 171
-accusations of apathy 172
-problems with endowments 178
-inheritance 178
-Dr Tuke's asylum 178-179
-restoration plans 182
-renovation and enlargement of the vicarage 184-187
-Stapleton House 186, 189
-library 202
-sequestration order 205-206
-death certificate 206

Cotton, Agnes 9, 154, 207
       Phoebe 9, 58, 93, 131-133, 149, 150, 154, 157, 159, 163, 165, 171, 207
       Sarah (sister) 9-10, 13, 85, 93, 127, 131-133, 150, 154-155, 159, 165-167

Covent Garden 169

D

Dale 106, 149
Danby, G Hammond 192-193, 196
Darwin, Charles 74, 78, 81, 222
Davies, Christopher 99, 121
      Richard 76, 80, 91-92, 108
Davis William 99, 121
"Deborah" 156, 161
Demerrara 38
Devil's Tower 54
Dick, Alexander 54
Dieffenbach, Ernest 71, 79-80, 222
Dixson Library 7
Dodgson, Charles 168-169
"Dolphin" 136
Douglas, John 183, 185-186, 189, 205, 222
Dudley, Reverend WC 34, 38, 48, 99, 121, 126, 139, 158, 171
Duke of Newcastle 11
Dull, John 198

E

E'Ongi 80
East Cape 96, 109
Eden Chapel, Overton 181
Education Act 204
Edwards, Mr 204
Endowed School, Overton 203
Epsom 10
Eton College 4, 10, 11, 23, 34, 220
Eton College (Waimate) 87, 99, 100, 102, 104
Evans William 34, 42, 44, 47, 59, 84, 148, 159, 222-223

F

Fairburn, Mr 109
Farmer, Mr 34, 44, 147

Field, The 201
Fisher, Frederic 34, 47, 99, 137, 138, 145, 147, 157
Fitzroy, Governor 122-123, 218
Five Crosses 181, 205
"Flying Fish" (vessel) 148
Forest Mere 220
Frodsham 3-8, 17, 162, 171-175, 177, 180-181, 184, 186, 190-193, 197-198, 200-206, 208-211, 218-219, 221
Frodsham Girls' School 201
Frodsham Grammar School 184
Frodsham Infants' School 203-205

G

Garratt, George 186
Giles, Reverend WT 206
Gipps Sir George 57
Glasgow 214
Gott, Mr 34
Great Tent 122, 138-140, 202
Great Bee & Honey Show 202
Greenock 34, 38
Grey, Sir George 156, 218
Griffith & Farran 200
Guildford 180

H

Hall Reverend 171-175, 180, 195
Hamlin, James 76, 86
Hau, William 91
Hauraki Gulf 216
Hawkins, Mary Eliza 126, 149, 160, 162
Hay, Messrs 180
Hazlehurst, Thomas 180-181
Heke, Hone 78
Heke, John 144, 146
Helsby 178, 182, 183, 197, 203, 204
Helsby Church 182

William Charles Cotton MA
1813 - 1879
Priest, Missionary and Bee Master

High Sheriff of Essex 15
Hitchin, Major 191, 196
Hobhouse, Eliza 165
Hobson, Capt RN 60-61, 216-218
    Lady 60-61, 88, 216
Hobson's Bay 138
Hogan, Helen 117, 119, 129, 133, 222
Hokianga 78, 88, 91
Holtzkaphelt 146
Hone Hika 78
Hongi Hika 75
Huddert & Co, Limehouse 15
Hugall, Mr JW 185
Hulme, Colonel 143
Hussey, Robert 34, 104
Hutton, Thomas Biddulph 7, 102, 106, 116, 121, 128-129, 137, 147, 157

I

Iron Church, Frodsham 180-183, 185, 194

J

"James" 88
Jamieson, Messrs 214
Journal (WWC) 31, 35, 46, 50, 52, 55, 64, 72, 83, 94-96, 98, 116-118, 121-
    123, 128-129, 131-133, 135, 137, 140, 152, 158, 159, 216
Judd, Mr 149
Judges Bay 59, 136

K

Kaikope 113, 114
Kakepuku 119
Kawepo, Renata 112, 114, 116, 118
Kempthorne, Mr 148
Ken, Thomas 92
Keri keri 68, 74, 76, 91-93, 97-98, 120, 129
King Island 51, 53
Kingsley 172, 174, 178, 179, 203, 204, 205, 222

Kohimarama 134, 152
Kororareka 75, 87, 144

L

Lake Omapere 76
Lake Taupo 114, 115
Lanes, Mr 193-194, 196
Leslie, Mr 34
Liberal Government 204
Linaker, WH 191, 193-194, 196
Lincoln 13, 24
Lincoln's Inn 220
Lisle, Mr 34, 47
Liverpool 180
Livestock 40, 43, 53, 142
Lowther, William 34, 47

M

Madan, Reverend George 173
Madeira 38
Magdalen Hall (Waimate) 100, 104
Mangungu 88, 216
Manley 178
Manor House C P School 8
Maoiri
    boy 34, 37, 38, 41, 45, 48, 56, 65
    language 36, 37, 38, 56, 120
    society 71, 72, 79
    children 101-102
    expeditions 112, 114-120, 148
    controversy 123-124
    Christmas Dinner 139
    rebellion 144, 146
    beekeeping 152-154
"Marian" 136, 152
Marsden, Reverend Samuel 74- 75

Martin Mary 34, 36-37, 39, 54, 56, 58, 59-60, 62, 64, 71-72, 81, 102, 115-116, 120, 122, 132-133, 135-136, 148, 153, 158, 159, 162, 217, 223
William 34, 59, 60, 105, 116, 148, 153
Matakana 138
Mata Mata 84
Matthews, Joseph 105
Mayd, Reverend W 10
McPherson, George 34, 51
"Medusa" 102
Mellish 12
Milland 220
Milner, Mrs EJ 208
Ministry of Agriculture Library 203
Mohi 72
Moneurs Island 54
Mosman's Bay 93
Myres, Reverend Dr 208

N

Napier, Lord 164-165
National Society 16, 204-205, 211
National School for Girls 181, 201, 203, 205
Nears Frederick P 191, 196
Nelson 84, 88, 117
Netherton 219
Newcastle Prize 11
New Plymouth 115, 117
New South Wales 7, 50, 52, 55, 72, 80, 83, 88, 94-95, 98, 104, 116, 118, 121-122, 128-129, 135, 137, 140, 151-152, 221
New Testament 108
Newton Heath 198
New Zealand Journal 123
Nga-pui 78
Nihill, William 34-35, 99, 107, 115
"Nimrod" 138
Norley 172, 174, 203

"North Star" 143
Northwich 192

O

Official Bay 153
Ohaeawai 76
Old Hummus 169
Otaki 117
Otana expedition 112-114
Overton 181, 197, 203-205, 219
Overton Collegiate School 192
Overton Hill 219
Oxford 4, 9, 12-14, 18, 34, 58, 87, 94, 124, 150, 157, 163, 167, 168, 170-171, 176-177, 182, 189, 209, 220
Oxford Apiarian Society 18

P

Pa Heke 111
Paihia 65, 68-70, 74, 91, 107-109, 135
Palmer, Caroline 33, 137
Papagay 201
Parakua woods 149
Paramatia 57
Paris 165
Parish of Frodsham 172, 202-203, 209
    collection of books 202-203
    endowments 172, 178-179
    townships 172, 173, 174
Parliament 143, 185
Parnell 138, 139
Paver, Mr 185
Peggy 202
"Penyard Park" 157, 161
Penzance 161
Percival, Mary 201
"Phillipson & Golder" 200
Pickmere, JR 194

Plymouth 25-26, 28, 32-33, 41
Pollard, John 190, 197
Pollard's Drapery Store 190
Port Adelaide 214
Prince, Mrs 146
Prince of Wales 201
Privy Council 220
Puketona 76
Purchas , Mr 157
Purewa Creek 135-136, 150, 152

Q

Queen Anne's Bounty Board 185
Queen Victoria 217

R

Rangihoua 74
Rangitoto 60
Reading University Library 203
Reay, Charles 34, 39, 47-48, 84
"Retrench" 38
Richardson, Sir John 24
Richmond , Major 23, 60, 70, 92, 167
River Mersey 219
River Weaver 219
Robinson, James F 30, 197-198, 210, 223
Rondondo Island 53
Rooksnest 127
Rota 96
Rotorua 84, 115
Roto Waitea 139
Rotu Mahana 80
Runcorn 4, 181, 191
Runcorn Board of Guardians 191
Rupai, George 34, 37-38, 41, 45, 48, 56, 65

S

"Schnurrdiburr" 198, 210
School Boards 204
Selwyn Dr GA 7, 20, 23-26, 28, 32-34, 36-37, 38, 40, 43-44, 47,
  51-52, 55-60, 63-65, 68-71, 80-85, 87-89, 90-94, 96-97, 99-102,
  105-107, 109-112, 114-116, 119-121, 123, 125, 131-135, 138, 141-
  142, 144-148, 150, 152, 156, 158, 160, 163, 222
    John (Johnnie) 100, 150
    Sarah 24, 26, 28, 30, 32-34, 37, 38, 65, 69-70, 80-85, 87-89, 90-
    94, 105-107, 109-112, 115, 119-121, 131, 138, 141, 144-148, 156,
    159, 160, 162-163, 170
    William (Willie) 68-71, 83, 89-90, 120-121, 150, 155, 223
Selwyn College Archives 155
Shortland, Lieutenant W 218
Sierra Leone 38
Smales, Gideon 216
Smith, Mrs 59, 140, 158
Society for the Promotion of Christian Knowledge (SPCK) 16, 223
Society for the Propagation of the Gospel (SPG) 64, 100, 102, 143
Sparke, Mrs 151
Spencer, Reverend FH 59
Spraltz, Dr 190, 191
Stack, Canon James West 106
Stapleton House 186, 189
Stapley, Ann 64, 120, 131
State Library of New South Wales 7, 50, 52, 55, 72, 83, 94, 95, 98, 104,
  116, 118, 121-122, 128-129, 135, 137,
  140, 152, 221
St Edward's Church, Romford 14, 20
Steele, Reverend Dr Thomas 151
St John's Church, Waimate 85, 93-94, 122
St John's College, Tamaki 86-87, 99-100, 103-104, 108, 109-110, 134-135,
  137, 143-144, 146-148, 150-151, 155-157, 163
St John's Collegiate School 98, 102-103
St John the Baptist Church, Leytonstone 17, 207
St Laurence Church, Frodsham 7, 172, 176, 177, 180, 182
St Mary Redcliffe, Bristol 165-166, 173

St Paul's Island 48, 50
St Paul's Cathedral 16
St Paul's Church, Stepney 16
Streatfield, Reverend Thomas 220
St Thomas's Church, Bethnal Green 16
Swainson, Attorney General 59, 148
Sydenham 202
Sydney 7, 28, 51, 53-58, 69, 85, 88, 91, 93, 144, 151, 156-157, 161

T

Tamaki 134-135, 138-140
Taranaki 112, 115, 119, 148-149
Tauranga 125, 129, 133
Taurarua 59, 115, 120, 136, 140, 162, 217
Taylor Mrs 83-84, 91, 111
       Reverend Richard 83-84, 91, 111
Telford, Mr 147
Teraia, Maori chief 60, 61, 71
Thames Valley 60
"The Flying Fish" 43, 214
Therapia 164
Tiley, Henry 191, 196, 201
The Times, London 123, 133, 171
"Tomatin" 25-26, 28-29, 31-40, 48-51, 54, 57-60, 65, 86, 88, 93, 131, 214
Torepo 84
Torquay 165
Treaty of Waitangi 158, 216-217
Tudor, Mr 147
Tuekett, Mrs 194
Tuke, Dr Seymour 178-180, 191, 194, 206, 208, 209
Tyas, Reverend 174, 178, 195

U

University of Oxford 170, 220

V

Vicarage, Frodsham 8, 181, 184-188, 190, 194, 200-203, 205

"Victoria" Government Brig 120, 135, 217
Virgil 9
"Vixen" 41

W

Wairau massacre 144, 159
Waitangi 76, 151, 158, 216-217, 222
Waitangi River 76
Waitemata Harbour 60- 61
Walwood House 9-10, 15, 154, 167
Warburton, Mrs 193
Ware Karakia 114
Warrington 193
Waterloo 201
Watson, Misses 94
  Mr 34, 47
  Reverend RP 201
  Robert 54, 55
Watts, William 64, 92, 107
  Mrs 47, 64, 100
"Wave" 63, 65
Wellington 66, 84, 115, 117, 132, 137, 154, 221, 224
Wesleyan Church/Chapel 88, 119, 181, 213
Whanganui 116
Whytehead, Reverend Thomas 34, 38, 47-48, 58, 85, 86, 91-92, 94, 99, 100-
    102, 110, 161, 223
Williams, Archdeacon Henry 65, 91, 95, 105, 109
  Jane 125
  Reverend Robert 73, 177
  Reverend William 87, 108
  Sarah & Catherine 73
Wilson's Promontory 53
Windsor Parish Church 20, 21, 22, 24
Wingate, Captain 214
Wiremu Kapa 113
Wolfenden Reverend Edward 173, 175, 195, 209
Woodford Bridge 165

Woodhouses 219
Woodyear 180, 182
Wright, Edward Abbott 177, 186

Y

Yate, Reverend William 76, 224